Picture It!

Teaching Visual- Spatial Learners

Betty Maxwell
Crystal Punch

Cover Design: Kate McPhee
Photos: Afsaneh Makooi

To Linda Silverman, who has made the world aware of the amazing strengths and special learning needs of visual-spatial learners.

Acknowledgments

In addition to being a wife and mother, I have loved teaching and learning. Most of my learning has been experiential, through schools, and then through my own practice. I had defining moments along the way, the hardest students were my best teachers. I have specialized in working with visual learners through my work as a Davis® Dyslexia facilitator, and my work and friendship with Betty Maxwell, and the teachings and discoveries of Linda Silverman and Ron Davis

I would like to thank my family for their support with my life long pursuit of how people learn. My children, Afsaneh and Milahd have been two of my best teachers, as have all of the students that I have been honored to work with. I want to especially thank my husband, Bijan for his love and support, and push to finish this book. He has kept me going with this project, reminding me of the importance of the work. Last, but not least, I want to thank Betty Maxwell, my friend, colleague and mentor. She kept me (a visual learner) focused with her kindness, sense of organization, spirit and boundless patience. Our intention is to shift our focus on the methods we use to assess and document the learning of Visual spatial students.

~Crystal Punch

I am grateful to all of my visual-spatial students whose struggles with reading, despite obvious good intelligence, have opened my eyes to the need for new ways of teaching them. I am also grateful to Linda Silverman and her Gifted Development Center for helping me learn about teaching strategies that work for visual-spatial learners.

~Betty Maxwell

Contents

Picture It! Teaching Visual-Spatial Learners?.....................9

Chapter One
Getting Started..13
Spatial Strengths..16
Mirror opposites...24
Picture thinkers VS Step-by-step learners.....................25
How to spot a spatial..31

Chapter Two
Retooling Your Classroom For Picture Thinkers..................33
Ten teaching tactics for classroom balance......................35
1. Give the big picture up front................................37
2. Use visuals generously....................................40
3. Provide models of expected products.........................45
4. Expand the visualization skills..............................48
5. Teach how to organize information pictorially...............53
6. Teach how to take picture notes as well as word notes......61
7. Imitate word processors in writing and editing..............64
8. Avoid timed tests-teach time awareness......................66
9. Increase complexity if focus decreases 71
10. Be upbeat. Let humor, appreciation, and positive..........74

Chapter Three
Visualization: Imagine that!..................................77
Getting ready to visualize...................................80
Classroom use of visualization..............................82
Visualizing in language arts.................................86
Visualizing for math..91
Visualizing for social studies................................95
Visualizing for science......................................97
Visualizing for sports......................................100
Visualizing for the arts....................................101
Other aspects of visualization..............................102

Chapter Four
Whole Word Reading..105
The phonics road bump..107
Strengths that work...112
Organic reading- Sylvia's way.....................................113
Organic to whole word...115
Getting started with Whole word reading.....................117
Playing with word patterns: Analytic Phonic.................122
Creative reading-another road bump............................132
The words-you-can't see road bump- the Davis way.........134
Making Bland words into wholes..................................139
The road bump of summarizing: finding the main points...140
Tongue Twisters for better blending............................144
Visualizing to spell..146

Chapter five
Math for Picture Thinkers...149
Working from right brain strength................................151
Those pesky math facts..153
100's charts and multiplication...................................162
Math vocabulary words..166
Picturing word problems..168
Showing your steps...170
Fractious fractions and their equivalents......................173
Negative numbers..176

Chapter six
Picture Yourself Teaching Writing to Picture Thinker......177
Writing from the heart...180
Living words...182
Still life with senses...182
Sensory stations..183
More ideas to stimulate the writing process...................185
Writing large to small...187
The magic of freeze frame..189
Wow, we can stop time!...191
Beginning, middle and end- organizing writing...............195

Freeze frame ideas to get started...........................196
Introducing a single frame or slice of time.....................197
Freeze frame: the picture thinkers time stopper...............200
Planning boards 201
Non-fiction writing for the picture thinker....................206
Write about what interests you..............................207
Sticky note notes...208
Using documentation boards to organize.....................210
Adding details with freeze frame notes.......................213
Freeze frame note taking....................................213
The picture writing process..................................215
Four big ideas for choosing a subject.........................217
Encouragement- a necessary ingredient......................220
Large ideas the freeze frame way............................222
Organizing the big ideas....................................225
Freeze frame picture notes..................................226

Chapter Seven
Time and Organization for Picture Thinkers.................229
Developing a sense of time..................................230
Estimated time V actual time................................230
Banking time...231
Planning that works for you.................................232

Summing It All Up.......................................233

Bibliography..237

Appendix...239

Picture It!
Teaching Visual- Spatial Learners

Why this book?

Picture It! grew out of discoveries both authors have made during their classroom teaching experience about how hard it is to engage and really help certain students. Both of us are good at innovation, listening, positive reframing, being supportive, and chaining up to successful experiences, but as happens for most teachers – there were students with whom we experienced failure. Nor did those youngsters feel good about the situation

Each of us, in time, and out of the classroom, met leaders who had created whole new ways of looking at how to learn. Crystal met Ron Davis, and became a Davis® Dyslexia Correction Program Facilitator. She directs Alternative Learning Solutions in Centennial, Colorado and has gained through her one-on-one experiences with unique learners (of all ages) a wide repertoire of techniques that work. Betty became involved with gifted education and is affiliated with Linda Silverman, Ph.D, Director of Denver's Gifted Development Center and pioneer in exploring visual-spatial learner territory. Betty is now Director of the Visual-Spatial Resource, founded by Linda. When Crystal and Betty met, it was synchronicity! We both clicked, complementing each other in vital ways and learning, learning, learning from each other.

We dedicate this book to those difficult students we struggled with. Bless them! They motivated us to explore new ways of helping children learn, based on new paradigms and the positive feedback these approaches have generated. We want to pass what we have discovered on to you.

Main Ideas Found Here:
There are two major ways of learning. The first is left-brain **auditory-sequential.** These learners easily follow others' verbal explanations and remember step-by-step directions, pay attention to details, naturally categorize, and know a mountain from a mole hill. The sequential way of learning is well-known to teachers. It is the traditional way.

The second way is right-brain **visual-spatial.** These learners (VSLs) are also known as picture thinkers. VSLs are more self-directed exploratory learners, who ask questions and look at a new subject from many angles. They make sudden, intuitive leaps, getting the idea all at once when they *see* it in their mind's eye. They think in pictures (images) and may need to search for the right words to explain what they know. In traditional classrooms, picture thinkers' needs are less understood and often thwarted.

It is possible to provide support and techniques for VSLs while still serving sequential learners well. In fact, this synthesis makes for a more vibrant and happy classroom. After all, it is the way our brains work best: both hemispheres thinking together.

Who is visual-spatial? There are many subgroups. Some are more creative (artists, musicians, dramatists, inventors, designers, lovers of fantasy). Some want to know how things work and take things apart to find out. Some are hands-on explorers. Some prosper in the spatial fields they have sought out (architects, computer programmers, surgeons, pilots, engineers). Some have some left-brain glitches but, given right-brain support, amaze with their creative solutions and grasp of significant ideas. Some are dyslexic. Some are highly distractible but can also hyper-focus. All, however, learn best when new learning is presented visually, specific steps are not required to reach a goal, and originality is honored.

What about children on the autistic spectrum? We have much more to learn about this area. There are autistic people who cannot create a whole from its parts, where most spatial learners do this extremely well. Spatial methods work well with some individuals on the spectrum, but not with all. Our jury is still out on this one.

VSLs may also be called picture thinkers, global learners, out-of-the-box thinkers, spatials, right-brain kids, or non-sequentials. We will use some of these terms interchangeably in our book. All point to the same need-set and the same great potential to enrich our world.

We hope you like our book. We would love to hear your feedback.

Betty & Crystal

Chapter 1
Getting Started

Let's begin at the beginning. What *is* a *"visual-spatial learner,"* anyway? What's so important about the visual-spatial learning style that's worth a busy teacher's time? Isn't this just another fad? Well, no. Visual-spatial learners (VSLs) have been with us forever and are here to stay. But they don't thrive in school. Lots of them feel stupid, even though they're often bright. Why is that?

This book is designed for teachers who are curious, who want to know more about visual-spatial students and how they learn, and who want to reach them and help them be successful. Understanding these students who "learning backwards" is important. It's ethical to begin with, just as providing special education for those with learning disabilities is important. In addition to being fair, it may also be a wise career move. Research has found one-third of students have this orientation! An even larger proportion may emerge in our electronic technological world where youngsters are immersed in visual games, TV watching, and even cell phone aps almost from the cradle. The art of conversation is giving place to texting. It is well known that verbal SAT scores have been dropping globally over the years while quantitative scores remain stable. We may be moving into an era where imagistic literacy becomes at least as important as being able to absorb the verbal content of a lecture. Expertise in the area of visual-spatial educational techniques is likely to become a highly marketable skill.

Research so far has found one-third of students in schools investigated to be visual-spatial learners. Roughly another 25% tested as audio-sequential learners — their opposite learning orientation — for whom most educational programs are well-designed. The remaining portion are a mixed bag, able to operate either and both ways: they benefit from getting the right brain Big Picture but can also focus on and remember all those left brain details. Linda Silverman, pioneer of investigation into the visual-spatial learning style and author of *Upside-Down Brilliance: The Visual-Spatial Learner*, insists that *all* learners benefit from teaching to right-brain (spatial) strengths. That's partly because much education has become exceedingly sequential, drill- and detail-oriented as the arts have been dropped from the curriculum. Attention to visual-spatial learning needs can restore balance to the classroom.

Visual-spatial learners (VSLs) are not new. These "holistic" or "right-brained" or "picture thinker" or "gestalt" (so many tags across the years!) learners have always haunted classrooms, giving teachers indigestion and gnawing at their consciences. They wonder: why can't I reach this obviously bright kid who won't catch fire? Educators often suspect some kind of learning disability. But VSLs should not be seen as disabled. Rather, they are differently able, often very able.

They have huge strengths that are usually not tapped, and their potential, when rightly engaged, is enormous.

Contrary to a common misunderstanding, the visual-spatial learning style is not just a preference for learning through seeing, not just a learning modality. Rather, it's an innate, right-brain orientation that involves the mind's eye in understanding the whole of something. VSLs generally prefer to use the mental visual "sketch pad" rather than the auditory "tape loop" to grasp and store information. This style interweaves creativity with emotion and significance as it organizes the world. In operation, it is fluid, dynamic, and experiential.

Traditional classroom teaching that uses linear, detailed, step-by-step explanations feels alien and dry to VSLs. The content "goes in one ear and out the other." VSLs don't respond well to prepackaged information or passive learning. They are actively curious people who want to investigate for themselves and figure out what something is all about. They want to find out how things work and why people do the things they do. It is easy for them to see relationships and recognize patterns, and they naturally want to use these strengths when investigating something new. They tend to ask many questions. They scan for patterns and imagine new combinations of things just for fun. Discovery methods work well for them.

Because they would rather explore on their own than be taught and are often unaware of their strengths and how to use them, VSLs tend to feel inadequate and frustrated in school. And they can be frustrating to try to teach. A better fit of teaching methods and natural abilities is needed. So let's consider what those abilities are.

Spatial Strengths

Visual-spatial learners have some remarkable strengths. They may not even know they have these strengths or think of them as strengths. That is because traditional classrooms tend to teach these right-brain students through their weaknesses and discourage them from applying their strengths—not intentionally, of course. It just happens because sequential strengths are emphasized in many classrooms.

VSL GIFTS

Vivid imagination

Visualization

Getting the Big Picture

3-D mastery

Seeing relationships

Pattern recognition

Out-of-box thinking

Radar scanning

Emotional intensity

Gamesmanship

Vivid Imagination

Visual-spatial learners (VSLs) are picture thinkers who live in their imaginations. Whatever they hear and talk about and even think about creates vivid pictures in their heads, and those pictures are usually on the move. These movies can include all the tricks of the movie-making trade: voice-overs, close-ups, split screens, panoramic shots, you name it. All their senses are involved. What they imagine is ultra-real to them. Ideas and situations and connections all play out in the twinkling of an eye on their inner TV screen. A lot goes on. We all know "A picture is worth a thousand words." Often VSLs become very impatient with listening to mere words. They are used to faster mind play.

Picture thinkers' spatial imaginations can run away with them in great leaps from one fantasy to another. However, when under control, there is almost nothing they cannot bring into play in the arena of their mind's eye. They naturally connect one set of images with associated images and ideas. They can learn to store these image-maps and pull out when they want to, a very convenient trick.

Visualization Skill

Visualization takes imagination a step further. Picture thinkers are wonderful visualizers (although some need to be reassured that it is okay to use this skill in school). Visualization is the most versatile tool in the picture-thinker tool kit. It can be applied to any kind of problem solving in life and used in all school subjects. It is really as natural as breathing for spatials.

There are two parts to visualization. There is the "cognitive scratch pad" that is like your computer screen where you draw what you "see" to use right away. Many call this "working memory." Then there is the long-term storage of visuals, much like computer memory, where images are stored to call up later. Both are powerful resources for visual-spatial learners. Images can include any or all of the senses, including the intuitive sense. They are not restricted to just vision.

Visualization is such an important tool that we devote an entire chapter to its wonders later in the book. There we include sample classroom activities that build visualization skills, and we show how to use visualization in a wide variety of school situations. Here, we are just want to emphasize how important this inborn power is for picture thinkers' success. Visualizing is helpful for all kinds of thinkers, but it is home territory for picture thinkers.

Getting the Big Picture

Perhaps this goes back to hunter-gatherer days. On meeting something new — a new experience, a new classroom subject anything unfamiliar — picture thinkers want to know right away what it is. (Friend? Foe? Food? Their ancestral urge kicks in.) Whatever the thing may be, they want to understand what it IS. This is not an easy process, but it is their way to learn. They know from experience that once they get the big picture, they can sit back and take in the details, all the bits and pieces that make up the whole of something. That sense of what it IS will be theirs forever.

To get the big picture, spatial learners need to ask questions. They are trying to connect the new thing to something they already know. They also benefit from being able to "look at" something from different angles. Processing time helps. Then the actual making sense happens all at once. One moment they are groping, struggling, even sweating, to get some glimmer of understanding. Then the moment — aha! The whole thing falls into place. This is why visual-spatial learners have sometimes been called "global learners." The whole comes first - then the parts.

3D Mastery

Although they may be called picture thinkers, visual-spatial learners don't just see flat pictures but view things in 3-D. They "see" ideas in depth, and are aware of many perspectives including bird's-eye and worm's eye views. They can rotate shapes in space and recognize a shape from a partial or oblique view. Their world is far more complex than flat worksheets or pages in a book.

At times, spatials talk about *feeling* their way through ideas. They grope through inner space as if they could touch ideas and feel what is there. This is the kinesthetic part of the VSL experience. They may gesture or move about to think better, draw in the air, or even look at things upside-down.

Seeing Relationships

Where sequentials naturally sort things into categories, spatials see connections. For them everything is interconnected, a seamless whole. They play with relationships and connect the dots of their environment in new and unique ways. They are attuned to relationships of all kinds — personal relationships, how-things- work relationships, cause-and-effect relationships, and even design elements. To them, experience is one big dynamic interrelationship. While they can do poorly on a multiple choice test — because they see possible ways in which each answer could be correct — they excel in divergent thinking and are open to a wide array of possibilities.

They also juggle in their mind how things might relate in new ways. All of this makes many spatials highly inventive. They easily brainstorm. Their creativity is habitual, making picture thinkers often appear spacey and absent-minded. Their absent minds are dreaming up the future.

Not only are visual-spatial learners highly aware of how things affect each other, they are keenly aware of interpersonal relationships. Their own relationships with other people are very important. They are often vividly aware of others' feelings and find that their ability to think and focus are affected by what others feel about them and how they feel about friends and others. When they have a good relationship with their teachers, their minds soar, and they learn exceptionally well.

Pattern Recognition

Picture thinkers have a special talent for pattern recognition. It's part of their awareness of connections, since patterns are recurring connections. Picture thinkers immediately recognize patterns that are pointed out to them. However, where they really excel is finding their own patterns. They often see connections among things that are overlooked by others. Once pointed out, the connections make sense to others who wonder why they never noticed that.

Affinity for patterns means that picture thinkers will learn math facts better through number relationships and pattern discovery than through rote memorization. Drill doesn't work for them, since their memories don't hold isolated, disconnected facts. They need to see the connections.

Out-of-Box Thinking

An important aspect in understanding picture thinkers is that they value originality. They think in their own way. Originality adds life and energy to mental projects, and picture thinkers want that zest in their lives. It is actually difficult for them to follow some one else's line of thought, especially if no Big Picture has been given first. Linear thinking is not the way their minds operate. After all, *seeing* takes in a whole 360-degree circle, not a line. Trying to walk a narrow line can lead to confusion, like walking a maze of canyons where you can't see where you are going.

Picture thinkers blaze their own thought trail. There seem to be no real steps but more an emerging grasp of relationships. Often they have a sudden insight that "of course! It all goes together like this!" Either slowly or in a flash, a whole concept emerges, and it may be brilliant or flawed. It is helpful to give picture thinkers a goal to reach and let them work an idea out in their own way.

Radar Scanning

Visual-spatial learners are always scanning their environment, taking in every little thing. Their radar is always on. They are alert for changes, movement, tones of voice, or shifts in energy. They notice if some little thing that was there yesterday is missing. They scan for signals that something is going to happen as well as for the general feel of things. What ever else they are doing—unless they are hyper-focusing, which is also possible—the scan system is sweeping, sweeping, with all antenna out.

There is another aspect to their radar. It also scans for what is meaningful, and out of this grows picture thinkers' organizational sense. Sometimes seen as having poor organization skills, VSLs have their own sense of order. It centers on *significance,* an emotional sizing-up of a situation to see what is important. Rather than order things top-to bottom the way step-by-step learners do—where main ideas stand out from less important details—picture thinkers respond to their **feelings** about importance. If something strikes them as worthwhile, it becomes part of their web of things to pay attention to. Instead of logical outlines, a picture thinker's scheme of reality is more like a 3-D star map. The various stars and stand out in different degrees of brightness (significance), shining against the dark space surrounding them and all interconnected in some way like constellations.

Insistence on significance and values is an important contribution that VSLs make to us all. "So what?" is their eternal question (among so many others). "What does that mean? Why is this important? Why should I care about this?"

Emotional Involvement

Picture thinkers live with their emotions wide open. They do not shut their feelings away to be examined later or put them to one side while they take a test. That is virtually impossible for them. Instead, their emotions enrich, interpret, and underscore their experience all the time. *Their emotions affect the way they think*. It is important to know that their moods intertwine with brain functioning. Their thinking can take off when they feel upbeat and confident and they will surprise even themselves with what they can do. On the other hand, if they are upset, confused, angry, or resentful, it's hard for them to learn much at all. It follows that picture thinkers tend to show great variability in their accomplishments.

When VSLs immerse themselves in something, they give their all. They put their heart into the situation, and what they learn becomes part of their life experience. Their enthusiasm about something can be infectious and inspiring. Their eyes sparkle, and it is hard for them to sit still as new ideas flood their brains. Or, if their sense of justice is stirred, they can become impassioned. If a situation being discussed is poignant, they can become deeply sad and need time to recover. Feelings matter to them. Compartmentalization is alien.

Gamesmanship

Picture thinkers love humor, fun, and excitement They were usually happy, fun-loving *bon vivants* as toddlers. Just as then, they have boundless curiosity, are natural explorers, and delight in discovery and excitement. They take naturally to playing games and are reluctant to accept that learning is a serious business. Their desire to liven things up, often by playing the clown or stirring up arguments, can be very annoying to a teacher with a lesson to teach, but they are (mostly) not behaving this way to be obstructive. They want life to be zestful.

Games and drama enable them to learn. They easily turn learning into play, inventing contests, skits, silly mnemonics, and all sorts of games. Often what they have trouble memorizing can easily be learned through some kind of game. Because they love using computers to learn (they are visual and have no time restrictions), computer games are a natural source of empowerment for them. Simulation situations also score. However, they like all sorts of strategy games and can easily turn something they are learning into a board game.

*   *   *

(Of course, there are many other minor strengths of visual-spatial learners, but we think these are the most important. We would love to hear from you what other strengths you discover in your spatial students, or perhaps are aware of in yourself. Contact us!)

Mirror Opposites

Visual Vs. Sequential

Another way to understand visual-spatial learners (VSLs), who are right-brain dominant, is to realize that they are, in many ways, the opposite of learners who are left-brain dominant, or *auditory sequential learners* (ASLs). Because they have always been the large group of traditional students in the classroom, ASLs have never been labeled "auditory-sequential." They have just been the students you are used to teaching. Investigation of the right-brain learner has been recent, so this contrast is also something new. We can think of it in several ways. We could use the terms "VSLs" vs. "ASLs" or call them "spatials" vs. "sequentials" or "picture thinkers" vs. "step-by-step learners." It's all the same thing. In this book, these terms will be interchangeable. Right now, let's use the last set of terms because it is the most picturesque and memorable.

Picture-Thinkers Vs. Step-by-Step Learners

Offhand, picture thinkers and step-by-step learners may seem to be two different species. However, the differences are better seen as complementary, each supplying what the other lacks. After all, they represent the two halves of our brain, with the left-brain step-by-steppers better able to handle time and details, and the right-brain picture thinkers better at grasping synthesis and significance. And, just as our brain works best when both hemispheres synchronize their talents, so classrooms are more vibrant and successful when teachers interweave both learning styles. This is not as tricky as it sounds, but actually is something most of us do all the time when we use our two-sided brains.

Step-by-steppers are good listeners.

They can follow a long trail of steps and details, storing the information in their excellent short-term auditory memories, and, at the end of the trail, the accumulated bits and pieces add up to a concept. (Or, sometimes, the whole concept isn't quite there, but they have the ability to go back and retrieve whatever information they need for a particular situation. They can also keep adding to the concept until they understand it). They can follow and remember long auditory explanations.

Picture-thinkers, on the other hand, are excellent visualizers.

They **see** what is described, making movies in their heads or creating mental structures of an idea. They remember what they see, conceptualize, or experience better than what they hear—unless what they hear is vivid and filled with images. That is why so many love fantasy and science fiction. Rather than follow verbally presented steps, spatials do better when they can look at pictures, models, or other visual representations of the whole.

Step-by-steppers can scan for the main idea.

Their minds outline: Here's the main idea; here are

these four supporting details. Here are the next most important ideas. These are the mountains; these are the molehills. They can actually sort out the high points of something and summarize the plot of a book or movie.

Picture-thinkers see all as a seamless whole.
So much is interwoven, so much is equally fascinating. If they are asked to create an outline or choose the correct answer on a multiple-choice test, they are at a loss. How can a statement be totally true or totally false? There are so many ways to look at the materials, so many connections to make. They easily recall an entire movie, including the dialogue, as if they were reliving their experience (which they are). Can they summarize? Usually not.

Step-by-steppers manage time and are better able to separate themselves from their emotions at will.
They have a good sense of time and its passing. They can work within tight time units, such as a 38-minute class period, pacing themselves to get a good amount of work done. Although they are just as emotionally upset when things go wrong, they have the ability to put their feelings aside to take a test or meet an assignment deadline. This ability to compartmentalize is often something on which they pride themselves.

Picture-thinkers, the right-brain learners, have their emotions bound up with their mental functioning.
When they feel good—they fly high, doing exceptional work. If they are depressed or angry, upset or confused, it is as if their brains turn to sludge and their work degrades—if it is completed at all. On the other hand, they will turn themselves inside out and do amazing work for a teacher who they feel "gets" them. Picture thinkers have little time sense. They do not budget time and have a very distorted sense of its passing.

Step-by-steppers thrive on step-by-step learning.

Helpful teachers have long broken complex information into small bits and easy steps to help students learn. They also often helpfully explain how to do assignments, step by step These students follow along, well able to defer understanding until the product is completed. Usually understanding accumulates for them as they work. Even if there is some confusion in their mind, they can recall those details and go over them again until it all makes sense.

Picture-thinkers need to have the Big Picture shown them up front.

Once they have the big picture framework, they can fit details in place and those details will stick. Otherwise, although picture thinkers can listen and understand in the moment what is being said, the details are likely to flit "in one ear and out the other." They have nothing to attach to.

Picture-thinkers also become edgy and ineffective if asked to follow directions when they don't have a picture of the goal.

Give them a model of the product or a clear goal to reach and they will get there in creative, often unique ways. Sometimes they find shortcuts. Sometimes they see the answer to a problem immediately and may not know how they got there. They do best when the end result, not the process, is the basis for a grade.

Step-by-steppers memorize terms, names, and facts well.

When asked a question, they can scan their fact banks and retrieve the information fairly quickly. They can think on their feet and spit out information readily. They make good Jeopardy players. They can sparkle in discussion and debate.

Picture-thinkers may have word retrieval problems.

For them, most knowledge is stored in image form or as some kind of spatial idea. They need time to translate their ideas into words. There are times when the words "are on the tip of their tongues" but won't come. Needing translation time can make them nervous when "put on the spot" by a question. If they initiate the conversation, their speech flows. When questioned, it may be halting.

Step-by-steppers often have excellent handwriting and take good notes.

They can learn to write quickly and to take readable notes. They can grasp what is important to write down because they have that mental template for outlining. Thinking and writing coordinate well in their brains.

Picture-thinkers struggle with handwriting.

Even when they are artists with well-developed fine-motor skills, their sequential writing skills are awkward. Their writing is often a scrawl or an atrocious mess. A few picture thinkers learn to draw their letters beautifully, but the process is time-consuming. Traditional note taking doesn't work for them.

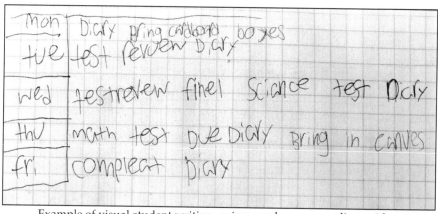

Example of visual student writing- using graph paper as a line guide

Step-by-steppers may need repetition to reinforce learning.

Their process often includes retracing their steps and deepening those neural grooves until a concept becomes clear

Picture-thinkers take longer to "get" a concept. Once the idea is formed and stored in image form, drill tends to erode it.

They strongly resist drill and repetition. If they are struggling with a concept, they are helped by new ways of seeing it. Repetition only frustrates them.

Step-by-steppers handle timed tests well.

They are able to memorize isolated facts, recall them quickly, write quickly, and do well. Often they enjoy racing against the clock.

Picture-thinkers dread timed tests.

Here everything works against them. Memorization of little units is foreign to them. Retrieval may be a problem. Their handwriting is not well-synchronized with their thinking and often interferes with it. Many fall apart when the clock starts ticking.

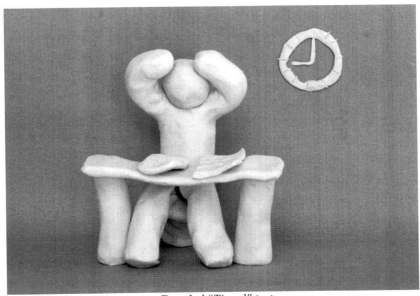

Dreaded "Timed" tests

Step-by-steppers are able to show their work and even write out explanations of the steps.

This task comes naturally to them, and instructions that ask for these steps are often quite helpful to them.

Picture-thinkers often have no steps to show.

They are Aha! learners, who often arrive at conclusions intuitively. They "see" the answers or are just aware of the relationships involved. Especially in math, asking for their steps is an exercise in futility. They should be given credit for their correct answers and asked to correct incorrect ones.

This Sounds Like a Lot to Learn!

These contrasts were set up to aid understanding of the visual-spatial learner, not to discourage teachers, who can immediately see some changes need to be made in their present classrooms. It is only because teaching methods have become rather lopsided, favoring memorization and speed (which ASLs do better) that this is so. What we are recommending are ways to restore better balance in how things are taught and learned, more in line with our own two-sided brains. It turns out that this is not nearly so difficult as might appear at first glance.

Before you turn away — it all may seem too complicated — think about this. We are talking about teaching to only *two* main learning styles. That's it. Just two. In the past, teachers have been urged to facilitate *three* learning modalities (visual, auditory, and kinesthetic), or absorb at least *four* major learning styles, such as Anthony Gregorc's four classifications, or subscribe to Howard Gardner's multiple intelligences, which have grown from *seven* to *eight*. And there are many other learning style patterns out there, vying for their attention. Talk about complexity and lesson planning! The Auditory-Sequential/Visual-Spatial model works with *two — that's only two —* major styles, and they represent the two halves of our brains that we are quite used to using together anyway.

The really good news is that **much of what works for picture thinkers helps step-by-step learners also.** Modifications to turn a sequential classroom (traditional model) into one that serves both major learning styles are not extensive. Although overly sequential methods frustrate VSLs, the reverse is not true. Making changes that are lifesavers for VSLs either benefit or have a neutral effect for ASLs. Important but not difficult changes can be made that improve learning for everyone.

That's why this book is written. It is designed to make learning easier for picture thinkers and their teachers (that's all teachers). The plan is to look at the most important things to know about visual-spatial learners, provide a handy tool kit of strategies that respond to their essential needs, and look at specific teaching tips for VSLs in the basic areas of reading, writing, and math.

How to Spot a Spatial

To be very clear, there is no dividing line between spatials and sequentials. Most students will have some traits of each, while there will be some who are more extremely spatial or sequential. There is no set of criteria to measure a spatial learner, but there are common sense observations to indicate that a student may really thrive using spatial techniques in your teaching.

Here are some clues about how to recognize those spatial learners lurking in your classroom. Some students have probably jumped out at you as you read the introductory material. Others may be camouflaged as goof-offs or space cadets or rebels or the ones that are just turned off. Certainly not everything listed below will fit any one picture thinker.

Traits of USLs

But here are some traits to ponder:

Picture thinkers may: be lost in space...seethe with impatience (a picture is worth a thousand words and is grasped instantly; everything else is slow motion) ...have terrible handwriting...have a wild imagination...hate timed tests, especially Mad Math Minutes...do math in the head and hate to write any of it out...have the right answers but not be able to show any steps (what steps?)...get math concepts but be poor with math facts and calculation...be good with maps, directions...draw or doodle while you talk...talk engagingly but write meagerly...know what's on the floors above and below them...know how to get anywhere they've been once...ask many questions...be absent-minded, lose everything...be The Mess!...take forever to finish assignments...know material but do poorly on detail-oriented tests...have strong emotions...be able to recite whole movie plots but not summarize...the main idea is a foreign concept...have original ideas, be inventive...may work backwards or start in the middle of a task... have poor phonemic awareness...guess at many words...be better with sight words...be forever late with projects...astound you with flashes of brilliance...think uniquely...search for words and gesture a lot...be rotten spellers...daydream...becomputer wizards...be oh! so sensitive...have sudden enthusiasms...be artists, musicians, actors, chess players, entrepreneurs...

When talking with the parents of picture thinkers, you may discover that as little tykes, they were Lego Kids, loved puzzles, and even put them together face down just by the shapes...continually built all sorts of things out of scraps and pieces...took things apart to see how they worked and could sometimes put them together again...remembered how to get places even when still in a car seat...saw shapes everywhere...were hard to pry away from the computer or gameboy... had rooms that were holy messes but knew where to find things in that mess. These parents may be engineers, architects, pilots, surgeons, artists, musicians, computer programmers, interior designers, stage directors, physicists, or highly successful businesspersons. Being visual-spatial runs in the family!

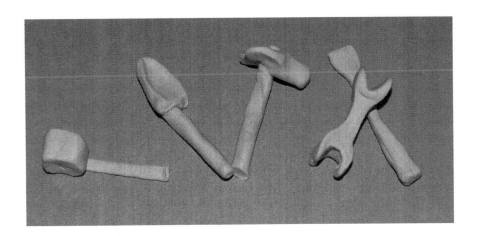

Chapter 2
Retooling Your Class for Picture Thinkers

What changes are really important to make a classroom user-friendly for picture thinkers? We have come up with Ten Teaching Tactics that make a huge difference for right-brain learners. They also add balance to the usually left-brain leaning classroom. Each Tactic is important, so do take time to read and think about how each works and how you might actually use it.. All are based on principles of right-hemispheric operation. Each requires full understanding to put into practice, because just going through the motions will not work.

Read about the Ten Tactics. Review them, digest them, and adapt them to your own teaching strengths. More detailed explanations follow the list, with examples and specific teaching ideas provided. Still more ideas and details for implementation can be found in Part B of this book. The Ten Teaching Tactics won't be upsetting for your sequential students — who will very likely enjoy them — but they will make a tremendous difference for your visual-spatial learners. As you read about each Tactic, picture yourself carrying it out in your classroom in your own way. Each Tactic adds to and complements present traditional teaching and rounds out the learning experience for all. Any Tactical step you take in the right-brain direction will be helpful, so don't feel that you need to do it all or all at once. In fact, it is fine, and probably essential to mental health, to take things slowly. It is good to begin on a small scale to see how these ideas actually operate. As the new dynamic becomes clearer and you see its success, you can enlarge its scope.

Some Tactics suggest that you acquire visual materials and models, which won't happen overnight, but this, of course, is a process that is good to begin. Suggestions for some resources are listed at the back of the book. Many student products can become teaching tools for the future. And materials you already have can be used in innovative ways. It's all in the way you present them.

Please don't worry if a particular Tactic is not clear to you right away. Several ideas are quite new but are really doable and helpful. Just keep on reading, absorbing, and visualizing yourself using these Tactics.

Ten Teaching Tactics
For Classroom Balance

1. Give the Big Picture up front.

2. Use visuals when teaching everything.

3. Provide models of all expected products. Credit the end product. Don't require a show of steps.

4. Expand visualization skills including how to store and retrieve images.

5. Teach how to organize information pictorially.

6. Teach how to take picture notes as well as word notes.

7. Imitate word processors in writing and editing. Cut/paste/add/reorder. Freeze Frame. Organize by graphics.

8. Avoid timed tests. Teach time awareness and management.

9. Increase complexity if focus decreases.

10. Be upbeat. Let good humor, appreciation, and positive emotions rule.

Ten is not so bad. In fact, most of these ideas are enjoyable to carry out. But they all take practice, and it is wise to try them yourself first to get their feel. Then start small and implement slowly. New ways always take some getting used to. These Tactics are going to be truly helpful to your picture thinkers, who have been swimming against the sequential current for a long time. They really *need* these changes. Sequentials may also like them, or they may prefer their usual way of operation. Both ways should be available to all students, a not-so-subtle reminder to everyone that diversity is valuable. This chart is simplified so you can post it where you will see it often and not forget these essentials to a fair, balanced, and dynamic learning climate in your classroom.

Now that you know what the ten teaching tactics are, the following section explains in detail what is meant by each of them. You will probably discover that you are already doing many things that are suggested. However, there are likely to be things, such as visualization, draw-ups, picture notes, and Freeze Frame that are new. There are exciting and powerful ways to draw out the strengths of your picture thinkers and also enhance learning for your step-by-step students. That's a win-win situation. There may even be things that raise your hackles, such as not requiring a show of steps if answers are correct or providing more complexity when a student consistently makes careless mistakes. Please be patient and read through to the end so that you can understand the reasons for these counterintuitive suggestions. They really do work.

After you have read and pondered and visualized each of the ten tactics in practice in your class, then we suggest pick and choose what you find yourself most in tune with. Begin there, and expand those practices first as you explore what works for you. It has to be plausible for you in order to work for your class.

It's actually good to go slow and take one step at a time. You may want to use that one step with one tactic tried out with a small group or even with one conundrum student. See how it works and objectively observe the results. Give it a fair trial. Each of these tactics is based on known strengths of visual-spatial learners and on overcoming known pitfalls for them. All are worth trying, It is very likely that you will be surprised if you were reluctant to begin with, or exuberant if you were enthusiastic about these ideas as you read them.

Each tactic is explained below:

1. Give the Big Picture up Front

This is a *key idea* for working with spatial learners. To remember details, spatials need a framework that provides a home in which the details nest. Without that framework, details are disconnected and really difficult to remember. New facts flit away. Spatials do not hold new information in their memories unless it fits a subject they already understand or connects in some way with established learning—something they can "see" holding together. Connections and relationships underlie the way they think. So give them an overview before teaching any details, and the details will stick like Velcro.

The Big Picture can be a visual, like a Place Value Chart that pictures the decimal number system. It can be a metaphor, such as "Organizing is like looking at a river system from an airplane." It can be an elaborate poster about ancient Egyptian society that shows the Pharaoh seated at the top of a pyramid, with the various social classes arrayed in order down to the vast number of slaves that make up the bottom of the pyramid. It can be a simple statement about what the goal of the day's work in a particular area is, such as "Today, we're going to find out what an electrical circuit is. We're going to put together some circuits." It can be a principle, such as "Dividing is the opposite of multiplying" — if students already know how to multiply.

Of course, VSLs may learn something new if it connects with something they already love, vibrates with significance, or captures their imagination (wild, cool stuff!). Of these possibilities, providing the Big Picture is easiest to do consistently. Establishing the Big Picture is also a sound educational principle, providing focus and clarity. Starting a lesson with an overview is an excellent teacher tactic. It helps the teacher show clearly the purpose of the lesson. It helps sequentials and spatials alike, and there are a variety of ways to do this. The overview can be a simple as a statement (something you probably already do),such as "Multiplication is really counting groups that are all the same, like four girl scouts each carrying 6 boxes of cookies. Would you really count every cookie to find out how many there are?" It can be a metaphor: A report is like a tree. The trunk of the tree is the main subject. The branches are the main ideas. The twigs and leaves and bird nests are all the interesting facts that make the tree fun to look at. See how the structure of the tree holds everything together. A report is like that, too." It can be a graphic symbol, like a pyramid: Look at this chart in a pyramid shape. At the bottom are all the slaves, whose labor made everything work. Then there are the artisans and traders. There aren't so many of those. Still higher are the soldiers, there to protect everyone from invasion. Still higher are the nobility, the privileged few. At the very top is the Pharaoh, the god-king. There is only one Pharaoh."

A Big Picture can also be fancy and fun. I read about and admired a creative teacher who greeted her class wearing a surgeon's mask and wielding a scalpel. She gestured over a large paper figure stretched out over her desk, announcing, "Today we're going to operate on the English language." A sentence does have parts that hang together and work as one, just as our body does. Those students *got* that language is a system with major parts (like a body's heart and head) and other appendages. They experienced it. The best overviews provide an explanatory picture.

On the other hand, the Big Picture needn't be complex or clever. Some teachers just write on the board, "Today we're going to learn the makeup of the heart and how it works." It isn't enough just to write "The Heart." That's not a goal. What is important is to remember to set up the Big Picture every time new information is introduced.

It's also helpful to remember that picture thinkers need to ask questions as they try to link the new information to something they already know. Whatever the question, they are actually asking, "Is it like this? Is it related to that?" They are trying to see what all this new stuff looks like. You can remind them that the Big Picture is just the beginning. As more details are given, the whole thing will take better shape for them. Encourage them to keep looking for those patterns they as so good at recognizing. And expect more questions.

Sometimes lessons are continued to the next day. The same Big Picture can be used again, even for the third or fourth day. Repetition of a Big Picture is okay. Suppose you are reviewing at the end of a unit. Consider an array of those Big Pictures you used during the unit. It should trigger remembrance of the contents for picture thinkers and step-by-step learners alike and provide the basis for a good review.

2. Use Visuals Generously

Pictures. Pictures. Pictures. All kinds of visuals should be used *as fully as you use your words*. You cannot have too many to support the picture thinkers in your classroom. Visuals often used can be hung on the walls. You can also use overhead transparencies to routinely supplement your verbal explanations. Visuals can be the symbols and squiggles you write on the board to clarify ideas as you talk. They can even be the way you write in the air and gesture to explain what you mean. Include pictures, graphics, models, maps, manipulatives, posters, diagrams, videos, computer programs, artifacts, charts, clip art, cartoons, demonstrations, etc. etc. Let the words you use be the kind that build pictures in the mind. Picturesque language also counts. The globe on the table and the time line running around the room are important visuals. The skeleton standing near the door is hard to forget. Platonic solids are available as wooden or plastic blocks to handle and think about during geometry class. Computer programs can provide dynamic visuals, as can videos and movies. Visuals can be memories of pictures and symbols previously used and recalled. The trick is to get used to giving visuals equal power with words. Picture thinkers need to see what you are talking about.

Many teachers like to set up bulletin boards that teach. Once the class gets used to displays with pictures, questions, and interactive answers, students or groups of students can create their own teaching bulletin boards as projects. These might even substitute for written reports. Teachers can draw up criteria for success with such a project (just one of many more possibilities for this kind of substitution), so that grading becomes easy with no surprises. Everybody benefits from such shared projects, and some are reusable in future years.

With your students, create webs or mind maps that out-picture the subject under discussion. These can be added to as you learn more. Use your chalkboard liberally. Use large chart pages to capture major points of class discussion (or type into your laptop to display later). Overhead projectors can be used to illustrate so many math situations, moving colored transparent bits around to represent everything from borrowing in subtraction to algebraic equations. Many sets of math manipulatives are available for this sort of thing commercially. Power Point presentations can make statements memorable. Collect and laminate pictures of all sorts. They can become story starters or illustrations for a point to make in science or social studies. Museums often provide artifacts for teachers to check out, many of which can be handled, so children can feel what a toddler's Native American beaded moccasin is truly like.

Don't hesitate to call up students to use as markers that represent points you are making. Several students can hold words on cards that, correctly ordered, make a sentence. A student volunteer — or the whole class — can decide where each should stand. Is there another way to order the sentence? Can you make the sentence into a question? You have just worked with sentence structure in a way that avoids writing. Maps, alphabets, number lines, and charts being currently used belong on the walls to be absorbed through much looking and use.

Models are really useful. These can be purchased, like the geometric solids mentioned above. They can also be teacher-made or exemplary student projects collected over the years. Lightweight models can be hung from the ceiling. This is a good way to display parts of a model sentence, color coded, showing the "bones" of the sentence and its main parts. Things that are used a lot, like number lines, the alphabet, or the periodic table of elements, need to be out and visible, and they already are in most classrooms.

It is possible to have chart racks where a collection of teaching charts are available for reference. Make these readily available. Materials can also be stored in 3-ring binders and albums, in pockets hung on the walls, in pull-out boxes stored on cupboard shelves, and on computer discs. A rich collection of visuals is a major step toward helping students build visual memory and visualizations that can be stored internally. These become the building blocks of visual-spatial thinking. Of course, this is an ideal to strive for. Most classrooms will begin with a few good models, but you only need a few good models to inspire students to create their own versions, as long as you allow these as class projects. A good way to begin is with game boards that relate to researched subjects. Students love to make and play with these, as example of real learning that is really fun.

Graphic Organizers

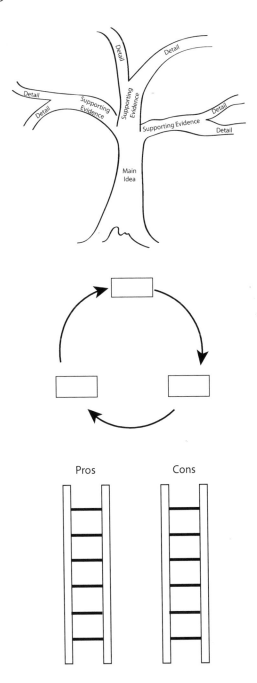

Graphic organizers deserve special emphasis. They are quite helpful to the writing process of picture thinkers (although they can also learn to create their own organizers) and to step-by-step learners also. Every classroom should have a packet of graphic organizers that are readily available to all who want to use them, and their use should become routine. The best organizers are simple and uncluttered, so that the basic design stands out. The simpler the visual idea the better. Students can always add to, elaborate, and complexify the idea; in fact, you want them to do this as they develop expressive writing strength.

Use dark, heavy lines if you are drawing your own organizers or look for commercial ones that a clear, simple, and helpful. You can also collect student-made organizers that are popular. You will need organizers for a variety of situations. Not only are they vital to show how thoughts and information can be structured, but, as you discuss stories and information with your class, you might also discuss how others have organized this material. It's great to be able to pull out a graphic organizer that fits. Or use your chalkboard to draw a visual of the story structure. Seeing the organization together with a story just discussed helps youngsters understand how important structure is to both art and science.

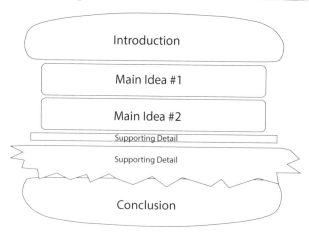

Graphic organizers provide a skeleton for the finished product and help the work hang together. A further benefit is that children come to realize that there are many ways to organize—even the same material. They learn to choose the organization that will work well for a given situation. This aids flexibility of thinking.

3. Provide models of all expected products. Credit the end product. Don't require a show of steps.

Picture thinkers need to see samples of what they are called on to do. They have listened to the words that tell them about the assignment, but they need to see what the end product looks like. Given that model or set of models, the creative juices start flowing, and they can begin to see how they can carry out a project in their way. Showing them is really important. There are many ways to do this.

For example, when working on writing paragraphs, you can post samples of good and not-so-good paragraphs on the wall. Add enlarged-print comments about good points and what makes them good. On a table, have books open with post-it flags marking well-written paragraphs. Rather than just go through how to build a paragraph with your class, which will appeal to sequential students, draw attention to complete paragraphs for your spatial students with color-coded components: lead sentence, details, bridging words, etc.

Keep examples of good writing. Sort them into stacks: "Vivid Descriptions," "Packed Sentences," 50 ways to say **said**," "Dialog That Moves the Story Along," and so forth. Encourage and expect students to add to these collections. Refer to them often.

Not only do all the steps of report writing, for example, need to be taught, but the process needs to be frozen in pictures, images, and written information at different stages that can be referred to and *looked at*. This can be as simple as binding together the transparencies used in teaching these ideas. These, and other visual aids, can be held in 3-ring notebooks stored for easy access to all. Model and encourage your students also to frequently check such resource material. This gets students out of their seats—a good thing—and makes them more active learners, another good thing to cultivate.

If you want students to keep lab notes and write up experiments in a certain way, provide them with examples as you teach, and make those examples easily available by posting them on the wall. Display sample lab reports with comments attached in large print. Identify all the parts you require to be included. Color-code them. Make a cartoon-like sequence of the steps to follow in an experiment (a kind of flow chart). Post it. Or project it from your laptop. You can use it to discuss what can go right and wrong during the experiment. If you want students to keep lab notes, jot some notes on the board as you teach, as an example. Encourage picture notes as well as word notes. (More about that technique later.)

Post sample notes and write-ups on the walls. The examples should include field drawings, sketches, and diagrams as well as words.

Videotape a well-done student interview. Project it and show it to the class. Enlarge and post good interview questions and ones that will lead nowhere. Post pointers from class discussion on what makes for a successful interview. Let dyads practice asking questions and getting information from one another, creating lived experience about what kind of questions are most productive. Discuss: what went well and what was hard about this. Discuss how to take a poll and show various ways of graphing results. Post them to be absorbed visually as well as used for ideas for real polls that students take and use.

Keep collections of examples of good writing. Sort these into "Vivid Descriptions," "Packed Sentences," "Dialogues That Move the Story Along," "50 Ways to Say Said," and so forth. Encourage and expect students to add to these collections and give them credit for their discoveries.

Collect outstanding student work and place this collection in a prominent place in your classroom. Laminate or otherwise protect each so that it can stand up to lots of scrutiny. Photos can be taken of superior dioramas and models. Photos arranged like story boards can illustrate plays or simulation games that students have created.

Keep good student projects to use as models from year to year. Keep several versions of a project and use as springboards for new ideas. If you have no space, keep photos of them in your computer to display when needed. You can see that this is an ongoing process, where your treasure trove will grow and become more complete year after year. Student products will be excellent assets and something other students will pay close attention to as possible for them to emulate.

4. Expand visualization skills. Create and retrieve visual images.

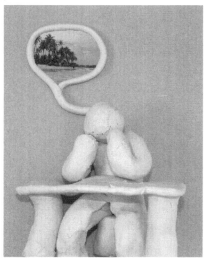

What a gift visualization is to the visual-spatial learner! So much depends upon supporting visual-spatial students' ability to visualize. It is their major learning tool, and its importance cannot be overemphasized. It sharpens understanding, aids memory, and enhances experience. It can compensate for weaker areas, such as the struggle with memorizing isolated math facts, dates, and terms, or trying to write both quickly and legibly. Visualizing is what spatials do as they think. In the theater of their mind's eye, they bring together images and ideas and see what can fit together to make something that is meaningful to them. Their images tend to be vivid, and they can build whole, elaborate collages of ideas and concepts. They can store these in their visual memory and call them up (eyes looking upward) when they want. But many spatials will be unaware that such mind play is a legitimate way of learning or that it can actually help them in the classroom. They may be used to being told. "Don't be a space cadet. Pay attention!" Making visualization an accepted, useful, valid classroom activity is like handing them their own passport to success. It is also a useful skill for sequential students to develop. It works for everyone.

Fortunately, there are many ways to introduce and build visualization skills in a wide variety of situations. Visualization enhances sports skills, makes writing more vivid and exciting, gives immediacy to history, provides an inside view of science where it can operate at a micro or macro level (you can see those chemical combinations happening or watch the Big Bang explode!), makes movies of problem solving, provides a view of possible outcomes to counter impulsivity, and even builds superior spelling skills.

Visualization helps students pay attention to details in their environment and see things from different points of view and new perspectives. It stretches their imaginations. It can make ideas much more clear and create a kind of lived experience rather than a dry storage of facts, which means that information is more usable in the future, ready to be merged with still more experience. It provides a whole new resource, useable for life. Visualization is to learning as vitamins are to health.

Visualization should be valued as an alternative way of thinking and used often. This can be as simple as asking, "How does that *look* to you?" "What do you *see* when you think about this?" "How do you *see* this coming together?" Such questions allow spatial learners to use their mental sketch-pad as a tool for understanding and are simple to formulate. It just takes remembering to do so.

Exercises and activities to develop visual memory and visualization are included in the material that follows. There you will find games that build attention to visual details and create more vivid images. How to access the immediacy of relived experience that makes writing vivid and lively make up another set of activities. Putting yourself in someone else's shoes can stretch a child's perspective and can be worked on through visualization. That also applies to thinking through or "seeing" the consequences of actions, a really helpful skill to develop. This chapter even includes brief visualization practices that can be tucked into the odd moment when the class is waiting for the expected visiting speaker to arrive or a period to end. Experience with storing and retrieving images and visually organized information is also included. Visualization can be as practical as helping to remember how to spell a "trick" word or as seminal as creating an entirely new way of looking at how people interact with one another and how that might change for the better. Don't forget to remind your students to look upward to retrieve these stored images.

Visualization is so important that schools are encouraged to act as a clearing-house for teachers' ideas for visualizations that works well. Shared school-wide, they will aid student comprehension and retention of information. This is one way to raise student scores on achievement tests.

Here are a few exercises to get you started. Some can be "time fillers" for those awkward moments when something has ended and you are all waiting for something else to start.

Take odd bits of time to develop visualization skills. Read a vivid passage to your students who have pencil and paper at hand. Then for 1-2 minutes, have them draw everything they can remember of what they heard. Now reread the passage and have them put tally marks at the edge of their paper for each detail they included. They even get a point for something they thought of but couldn't draw (maybe it was on the other side of the house and not actually visible in their drawing). Do this exercise often so that each child can see how they improve at this skill. An added benefit is that you build appreciation for many writers' great descriptive skills. This is also a good "settling" exercise to use when students first come back after a lunch break or recess.

Take 3-5 minutes to play Memory Lane. It goes like this: "Walking down Memory Lane, I smelled the smell of hot asphalt on the city streets in August." "Walking down Memory Lane, I heard a baby burp. I could feel the first slowly falling snowflakes of the winter touch my cheek." Any statement that evokes experience can be used. Make the point that visualization applies to all the senses, and images can be odoriferous or tactile, etc. Students close their eyes if they wish and let themselves experience what they heard. They can also contribute ideas for Memory Lane. Like all creative work, this activity tends to create good vibes in the classroom.

Take a moment, quite often, to suggest that the class "get a picture of what that (idea, behavior, statement) looks like" whatever *that* may be. It helps for students to share the way they see this thing. There are so many possible images! This is a great way to enhance class discussion. "What does the pattern of multiplying look like to you? What is the picture of caribou migration that you have?"

Encourage your students to "make movies" as they read, seeing what they read in their mind's eye. Talk about the visual details they "see" in this way. How does Spot run and what does she look like running? Can they see the dew glistening on Charlotte's web? Just what color is Becky Thatcher's hair? An excellent way to improve reading comprehension is to stop at the end punctuation of a sentence and visualize it. What just happened? What did you learn?

Play any of the visualization games in *Put Your Mother on the Ceiling* by Richard DeMille. You can change it to *Put Your Teacher on the Ceiling* if you like. These silly exercises usually induce giggles and raise the good feeling level of a classroom. You can't not visualize what is suggested anymore than you can't not grimace if you "taste" a slice of visualized lemon.

Remember to use the words "see" and "look" a lot. They invite the visualization process. You will want to say things like, "Do you see what I'm talking about?" "What does that look like to you?" or "Can you see how that works?" When I mention panning for gold (or whatever) what do you see in your mind?" Share the different views of things.

Whenever students write, they should get into the habit of *seeing* in their mind's eye, whatever they are writing about. If they take a brief time to visualize their subject, their consequent writing will be much better than if they just plunge in to their subject.

This stuff really works!

5. Teach how to organize information pictorially

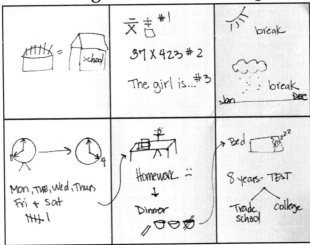

Excerpt from a report on China

The idea of organizing information with pictures may be new to almost everyone, even to some teachers. We do a thorough job of teaching students how to organize words into sentences, paragraphs, outlines, and compositions, but generally we do not do this with pictures. Yet this is a key skill for picture thinkers to acquire and master.

Mind Maps

Creating webs or mind maps to organize information has become fairly common in many elementary and middle schools, thanks to the innovative work of British psychologist Tony Buzan, who wrote *Use Both Sides of Your Brain* back in *1974*. Buzan used brain research on memory and learning as a basis of his work and wrote mainly for the adult business and professional world. He made waves in Britain, in Europe, and in the United States. In 1991, Nancy Margulies carried his work onto the young student level with her book, *Mapping Inner space: Learning and Teaching Visual Mind Mapping*, which is full of really helpful ideas about picture-based organization.

Tony Buzon used a spider-web lacework of lines and mostly words, often color-coded, Nancy Margulies introduced the idea of using mostly pictures and drawings, although she also used connecting lines and words. Both ways reveal the framework of an idea or concept. We highly recommend both Buzon's and Margulies' books for teachers. Together they lay the basis of creating organized picture-based concepts that fit the way visual-spatial learners think.

Mind mapping can be seen as a kind of graphic organizer that you create for each subject you want to remember. Mind maps, or webs, are a great way to introduce students to pictorial organization. A web shows how ideas are connected and which ideas are most important. It can be done with words, but it can also, as Margulies demonstrates, be done with pictures and images, using a minimum of words. A computer software program, "Ingenuity," makes web ideas available from the cybersphere for adults and high schoolers now. There is a version for the younger set called "Kidspiration." Both are available at www.inspiration.com. A mind map lets you *see* an idea as synthesis and in detail all at once. You can carry it around in your memory and call it up at will effectively. There are many ways to create mind maps. What works best for a given individual is what that person should use.

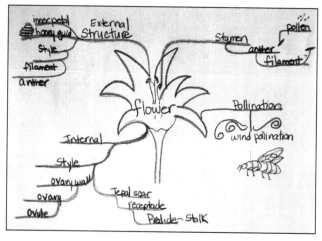

Posters

A second basis of image information organization is the teaching poster. Luckily, wonderful posters chock full of information are available from bookstores, public TV stores, teachers' supply stores, museum outlets, etc. The posters are about many things: different forms of cosmic nebulae, varieties of snakes, how to make cheese, components of weather or the operation of a turbine. They tend to be well designed and colorful, which is the point. You may already have begun a collection of these to pull out at the best teachable moment and then to post on the wall when a particular subject is covered. Such posters are great in helping students see how pictures and words can be arranged so that important information gets across and is memorable. Important things stand out, yet it is easy to find the details. Samples of such posters help students develop a sense of layout and esthetics.

Still another example of image management is the all-too-familiar ad. Advertisements are made to be memorable, and students can learn a lot from analyzing their construction. You may even have done a unit on persuasion and how ads manipulate our feelings and have material from that unit. Help your class collect and examine a variety of ads to see how the big ideas are centered in images but how crucial slogans and pictures are also included to create a whole message that stays in the mind. What makes some ads more dynamic? Which stays in your mind best? Which makes remembering a lot details easy? How would you create an ad to make the story of "The Three Little Pigs" utterly unforgettable? Help your students discern how ads work. Incidentally, students can learn the power of images to persuade at the same time—another good teaching idea. In doing this, you are helping build image-organization skills.

Draw-ups

Image organization is so new, in spite of these examples, that there really isn't any good name for the process. Mind mapping comes closest, but the idea needs to go beyond just one technique to allow for individual needs and creativity. While working on this section, I wracked my brain to come up with a generic term that would work. I thought of "Info-posters" but often smaller units than a whole poster need to be created, and that term sounded too ambitious. I thought of Picto-schemes, which came a bit closer. Then I hit on "draw-ups," comparable to "write-ups" that are done in words. It seems general enough and stretchable enough to serve as a usable term, at least for now. So, in this book, I'll use the term "draw-ups" to stand for the visual-spatial need to draw and organize information in pictures, useful in so many ways.

How do you teach your class about draw-ups? It is important to have lots of models on hand. This would include a collection of posters and ads. You can also point out examples of image organization in textbooks you are using.

Most texts include charts, graphs, and symbolic pictures. Think of the Food Pyramid, or state maps that show visitors' "Spots of Interest." Murals, an art form often found in social studies texts, show how historic events can be pictured symbolically. Science books are another good source of diagrams of specific information. Information visuals range from the very linear 2D form to the dynamic 3D vivid attention grabber (pop-up books are one example, but even better are the short videos you can run on your computer or cell phone), and you will want to have a variety of examples to illustrate the many possibilities. Draw-ups can draw on all these, as well as doodles.

The next step in discovering the usefulness of draw-ups is a class project in making them. Be sure to stress that good organization, not polished art, is the key here. Not everyone is an artist, and it is important to be able to sketch draw-ups quickly. Otherwise, they are like a piece of writing with every letter beautifully drawn but saying little. They should become an instant mode of organization: equal to thinking in outline form. You are aiming at allowing your students to organize their ideas and understanding in either words or pictures. Some will prefer the outline. Some will prefer and be better at the draw-up and find image arrangement appealing and useful. Draw-ups are just another tool to help our brains understand and remember. Learning how to create them provides balance in the classroom between left and right brain hemispheres.

Begin with something everyone knows, like the "Three Little Pigs" mentioned above. Go over the story with the class to be sure that everyone remembers the details, and then turn the class loose sketching the story. It all needs to fit on one piece of paper. However, do encourage your students to cut and paste good small sketches in place after designing the best organization. Discuss various results and decide together on what makes a draw-up work best. You may come up with things like this:

-Clean lines
-Emphasis of big against small items
-Good choice of a few words
-Inclusiveness. Everything important is there.
-Ease of visualization. You can close your eyes and see it.

During a field trip or while viewing a video, encourage students to quickly sketch what they are learning. They will need field notebooks, small clip boards, or some other good writing surface if they are away from their desks. Warn them that they will need to listen very intently in order to hear what is said and also sketch or doodle about it. Join them by doodle-drawing yourself. Afterward, have them see how they might organize all they gathered into a helpful draw-up. They can refine some of the drawings if they choose, but they don't need to. The idea is not to be neat but to be memorable.

Another way to work is right after a field trip or video viewing. Have a session in which students construct visuals representing what they just learned. There will be quite a variety of results. Discuss these. What was hardest about this assignment? Did some secretly make a mental outline to help the organization process? That's okay. It's natural for more left-brain dominant students. What was easiest? What kinds of emphasis do the different write-ups show? Which ones have the most information? Can anyone see how his or her own write-up might be improved in another try? Stress that many ways of organization are valid, but the focus is important. It is what you feel **must** be remembered. There is no right way to do draw-ups. They are personal, and they work if they help you remember something.

It will be important to go through this process several times during the year, because write-ups, like outlines, take practice and get better through use. You might also post a variety of your own draw-ups containing class information or samples of posters that show new ways to organize information. As you help your students grow in the creation of draw-ups, you are working toward situations in which outlines and draw-ups will weigh equally in the grading process, evening the playing field for the spatial learners in your class.

The more familiar and adept picture thinkers become over the years with doing draw-ups, the sooner they will reach a point where they begin to construct them directly as a visualization—just as some of your students already think in organized sentences and paragraphs. This process then becomes a viable way of listening to high school and college lectures and storing vivid, meaningful segments in visual memory.

Mental storage of draw-ups and other visuals
Storage and retrieval of visualized material has probably already begun if you have introduced your students to visualization spelling techniques. They have routinely been visualizing the correct spelling of words and calling them up in their visual memory by looking mentally upward. The exercise of having your class listen to descriptions and then draw what they remember of what they just heard also builds good recall of images and specific details. Both of these activities are great ways to practice storing and retrieving images. Playing visual memory games, such as "I Spy from Another Place" also builds memory and retrieval. Take your pick or invent your own lead-in.

Whatever you do, be absolutely certain your students know the rules of retrieval. The first thing to learn is that anxiety gets in the way. You will probably need to practice some calming exercises, breathing slowly, relaxing, and practicing an inner smile—or whatever works for you and your class — to provide that important tool. The second thing they know is to "look up" for their images. Visual memory is accessed, as neurolinguistic practitioners (NLPs) know, by looking upward. Some students may look up to the left, some to the right, but all will need to look up. That is where we human beings look to call up images. Students need to know that if they are upset, afraid that the word won't be there, or think they have forgotten, they are likely to panic and feel unhappy. If they stare glumly downward, they will not find the word on the floor. Then they will think visualization doesn't work. Teach them to calm themselves, breathe deeply, and look up. Up is where the image will be.

Visualization of spelling words or chemistry formulas or any other image memorization takes practice, just the way writing or tying shoes, or keyboarding all take practice. So help your class to practice storing and retrieving images by using many of the activities found in the Visualization chapter. Try a variety of them and keep using what the class responds to best. Talk with them about individual differences, and ask what is working best for each one. Variables that aid success are:

-Taking time to fix the image in your memory in the first place
-Knowing where to look to retrieve
-Mood
-How big a chunk of information you can handle at one time
-Other things like hunger, sleep, and self-confidence that affect all skills.

Your aim is for each student to learn what actually operates best for him or her.

As picture thinkers begin to retrieve larger chunks of material, they will want to experiment with what works best for them. Does color coding make a difference? What about enhancement of the image? When they first put their picture into their inner computer, are there parts they want to emphasize? Just as with spelling words, it's possible to use fluorescent color, have portions jump up and down and wave, or do a "zoom in" to enlarge parts that might be forgotten. As children gain experience, they will become more and more savvy about what they can include on one "page" in their mental computer. The habit of automatically organizing information into a visual format will be increasingly vital to spatial learners throughout school, including college, and will be important all of their lives. This asset just needs to be recognized as such and used to become a basis of success for them.

6. Teach how to take picture notes as well as word notes.

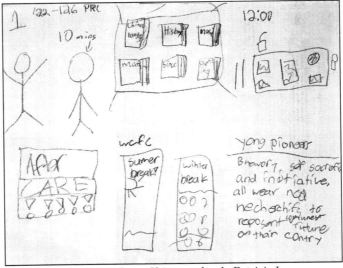

Picture notes about Chinese schools-Patricia Jones

Along with the use of draw-ups to organize large chunks of information comes the idea of taking notes using pictures, symbols, and colors, and other visuals to capture smaller chunks. Picture notes really work for VSLs. It is important to let them know that this way of gathering information is okay in your classroom, and even valued by you. Otherwise, they may feel they are breaking the rules if they do this. In the past, they may have been scolded or even ridiculed for "doodling" when they should be collecting information the word-based, or traditional, sequential way.

Picture, or visual, notes include ways for picture thinkers to doodle or draw pictures or use "idea traps." These will, according to the individual, hold information temporarily until it can be transferred to a draw-up or other informational synthesis. The usual note-taking methods do not work for picture thinkers for several reasons. Their writing is often an unreadable scrawl, or, if readable, very slowly done, so that major information is omitted. It is observably hard for picture thinkers to think and handwrite at the same time. Their hands tire easily and even cramp in the process. Drawing is far more comfortable for them. Allowing them to doodle or draw picture notes is not, therefore, a way to lose attention but rather to sharpen it. Spatials can easily draw or doodle and listen to new ideas at the same time. So let them draw. It's fine if their drawings are scribbles as long as the scribbles are meaningful to them. Ask them to use the scribble to tell you what they just heard, if you are skeptical.

Picture notes may begin with free doodling, so that the student develops a habit of having a pencil moving while listening. It is essential to allow students to doodle and sketch while you are teaching. When you finish talking, encourage students to draw a more complete picture (draw-up) that encompasses the most important things they just heard. You can check with them individually why they chose it what they did. This provides you with wonderful feedback about their understanding of something as well as helping them learn to listen for what is most important. Be open to their ideas; their pictures have to work for them. Be willing to help them fill in gaps if needed. Discourage "artful" drawing. This work must be done quickly to be most effective.

Word traps come from speed reading courses that often teach readers to jot down a keyword at the end of a paragraph, underline it and draw one to three slanted lines to "trap" other associated words. The idea is that you will then have a unit of information—a keyword with supporting details about what you just read. For example, if you read a paragraph about camels, you might write this:

[Camels; 1 hump Dromedary - 2 humps Bactrian]

A picture thinker might just draw a B on four legs and a D on four legs to store the same information. Later the words "Bactrian" and "Dromedary" might be added, if needed for that person. In most situations of listening rather than reading, few word additions are needed because the picture thinker is really listening, trying to decide what to draw, and concentrating strongly enough to remember what she just heard. The pictures just jog the memory.

Picture note-taking is very idiosyncratic. Each VSL will do it in her or his own way. Some will develop an elaborate system of symbols, abbreviations, and sketches. Another will simply draw a picture that fits the information he is hearing. Still another will doodle but add dates, terms and words here and there. For picture notes, the proof of their worth is in how well they aid memory. Although it seems counterintuitive, the large majority of VSLs can look at a picture drawn during a lecture and recall most of what they heard. It is as if drawing and hearing melded into a single, multimodal unit.

In our experience, VSLs are very open to taking notes in pictures. They just need permission to get started, and then practice to become quite good at this. It is good to begin in the third or fourth grade (or even earlier), and spatials will then expand their skills here just as they do in all other areas as they move upward through the grades. It is important for teachers to remember that sequentials may prefer using their words to capture ideas and find that word notes and outlining works better for them. Both ways are equally valuable and both require practice to gain mastery. Give your students their choice and let them discover which rewards them more.

7. Imitate word processors in writing and editing.
Cut/paste/add/reorder. Freeze Frame. Organize by graphics.

Writing by hand is almost universally awkward and laborious for visual-spatial learners. Why is not known, but we suspect that coordination of the parts of the brain brought to bear on this task is more difficult for them than for sequential learners. Auditory-sequential learners do not seem to struggle with handwriting. They generally learn to write legibly at a speed that serves them will in task completion and note-taking throughout their school career. Not so VSLs!

This does not appear to be the result merely of poorly developed fine motor skills. We have seen children who are artists and happily draw detailed pictures for hours on end struggle with writing sentences. It is an obvious effort for them. They tend to shake their hand often. Sometimes the hands physically cramp during the act of sequencing the letters in each word and the words in the sentence correctly while trying to remember what they want to say. We suspect coordination of right brain creative thinking with left brain sequencing needs requires a huge amount of effort, more than anyone suspects. We hope that someday neurologists and brain researchers will investigate this phenomenon.

Whatever may be going on, VSLs often avoid written work like the plague. They also much prefer to do mental math than to write numbers and think at the same time. When called upon to write stories and reports, their written sentences are as brief as possible, and often their writing is barely legible. Sometimes they do have beautiful writing, but it takes them a long time to produce it. We think they are actually drawing rather than writing, calling on the artist in them to create lovely letters.

Additionally, VSLs have a fast and furious idea flow, making it difficult for them to hold an idea in focus long enough to put it on paper. Consequently, they tend to omit endings of words or whole words and phrases as they write. The whole business is a struggle for them.

In another section of this book, "Writing Power," we have included a chapter on how to teach written expression to visual spatial learners in ways that make end runs around these problems. Please read it to understand what really works for them, hooking them into discovering their strengths in writing, which are vivid imagery, strong expression of feelings, excellent description, and the ability to make their ideas interesting. A different from usual approach is needed to unlock their potential inner writer.

Here, we are focusing more on the editing of writing. These ideas will work for VSLs and for every student, although some may prefer their usual mode of editing. In our opinion, students should know that there are choices and should be allowed to choose the method that works best for them.

Briefly, writing goes better for picture thinkers when they use their ability to hyper-focus on their writing and when they can physically cut, past, or sticky-note the arrangement of their writing, rather than create word outlines. Editing works best when parts of writing are polished and then physically assembled into a next to final draft (just as you can do with a computer). This penultimate draft may look messy and odd, but being able to arrange parts spatially really works. It not only fits the way spatials think, but the act of physical arrangement of parts is fun for them and sparks their creativity.

So, read the writing chapter, and stock your classroom with scissors, glue-sticks, colored markers, and tape. Cut and paste is not just for kindergarten. It is an integral part of computer-based editing of writing.

8. Avoid timed tests. Teach time awareness and management

Robert Ornstein, in his 1997 review of brain hemisphere research, *The Right Mind: Making Sense of the Hemispheres,* explains that the right brain has evolved to manage synthesis and overview, while the left brain works best with sequence and time sense. Hence, right-brain dominant individuals (VSLs) often have little sense of the passing of time, if any.

Even adults who are more creative, original and right-hemispheric struggle with time management. Most develop their own tricks and strategies for organizing their lives but often need help from others also. So VSLs do usually need help to better develop their sense of time. They do not do this well on their own. Here are a few ideas about how to help.

Allow plenty of time

Timed tests work poorly for picture thinkers. They emphasize all the areas of weakness and bring them into the public limelight. In the first place, picture thinkers struggle to memorize isolated units of information, like math facts and dates, which are usually the subject of such tests. They need a' framework to hold and make sense of the facts, so that the relationships can be viewed. They benefit from tests that use word math problems and give credit for correctly solving the problems. Such tests actually involve the application of math knowledge, and are a more complete measure of math mastery. Gaining automaticity with math facts is better done through playing games that involve knowing these facts (see the chapter on spatial math in this book) or playing with the multitude of patterns that emerge from a math lattice of any kind. For example, see what "Mr. Numbers," Tom Biensanz, does with math patterns on his website: eztimestables.com

At the very least, if timed tests for math facts is engraved into your curriculum, allow the picture thinkers in your class to mark their tests with a given symbol to show where they were at the end of the time period, and then take their time to complete the test, turning it into a power test, a better measure of what they actually know without the element of time being involved.

Time signals

During each class, set up a system of sounds that the class understands to signal: Half time. Fifteen minutes to go. Five minute warning. Stop. Prepare for the next session. Take three or four minutes at the end of the class period to ask, "Did you get done what you planned? Who knew when the half-time signal would go off?" Our technological age has now come up with something called the Time Timer, available from many sources, including Amazon. It comes in several forms, one of which is a projectable clock that can be set for a given period of time, say 35 minutes. As time goes by, the portion of the clock covered to mark 35 minutes recedes. You can literally watch time pass with this device; it clearly shows how much time is left for a given task.

You can also help students to build in a better time sense through exercising it. Every once in awhile, set this little task for your class. "Without looking up at the clock, see if you can tell about what time it is." Write your guess down. Then let them look up. If you have time, briefly discuss how close individuals are coming, how they think they are doing that, and whether any are getting better in their judgment of time. You can also see if they can tell how long a minute is. Start them with a sound signal. Have them raise their hand when they think one minute has elapsed. Then give a sound signal at the end of the minute. Paying conscious attention to time's passage helps to increase a better sense of it.

Vertical charts
Vertical visuals (you can't avoid seeing them) are the key here. Such a visual should be eye-height, clear, simple, and unavoidable. One such chart is the space where the week's assignments are displayed. This can be a permanent wipe-off chart with blank spaces for current assignments. Maybe in the near future, getting assignments will be as simple as snapping a photo of the day's assignment with a cell phone on the way out the door. In the meantime, the assignments are there in the same place, clear and current.

Project charts are another vertical visual tool that works well. At the beginning of the year a form can be created with a class roster listed in the left-hand column. Other columns list steps in the project underway. As class projects come up, the same basic form can be used, providing continuity but many variations. The name of the current project goes at the top along with a brief description of what is wanted. (Models of similar completed products hang to the right of the chart or are available in a handy notebook or album.) Columns can be set up for the various stages of the project. Each student fills in information as completed from her own project worksheet, such as project title and what it is about, various stages of collection and organization of information, layout, first presentation of material, critique, final layout—whatever a teacher wants to emphasize. Students write in the information as stages are completed. The chart can list what should be accomplished in the first week, at the quarter-way mark, the half-way mark, the pseudo-due-date, the actual due-date, etc. A glance at the chart provides immediate information of where everyone is on the project, which in itself, is motivating. Students can confer with each other because it is easy to see who has accomplished what and might have tips to offer. The more this structure is used, the more comfortable the sense of time flow becomes, especially if brief discussions call attention to the time sense each student is developing during the process. "How well did you plan for Part A? Did you give yourself enough time?

Color Coding

Color code your charts. Try red for the final due date, blue for the first decision point (specific focus), orange for the half-way mark, purple for some other important date. Use your own colors. Just be consistent from project to project. It is also a good idea to use the same color scheme for individual student materials as you deal time-sensitive situations.

In upper elementary through middle school, provide each student with 3-hole punched schedule forms, the simpler the better. Take time at the end of the class to fill out whatever information is required about the next assignment.

Experiment with the amount of time your class needs in order to do this completely. Encourage your students to color code also, marking most important things with their color of choice to stand for Attention! Don't miss this!! These then go in their notebooks, which hopefully are color coded also.

Plan B
Sickness, interruptions, emergencies, and mishaps happen to us all. It is a good idea to help certain of your perfectionistic students enlarge their planning to include a contingency plan.

What if the dog really does eat your homework? What to do then? Plan B should be a simple version of Project Plan A, which may not scintillate but may do in a pinch. Plan B may be a minor part of Plan A, which can be pulled out in an emergency. For those students who never do come up with an idea for a project, it is a good to have a Plan B file with already planned projects. It should be clear to everyone that Plan A projects to not earn the top grades that Plan A projects might. They are just a way of acknowledging that life happens. Students who use Plan B often obviously need counseling help.

Time Savers
Encourage sharing of time-saving tips. And, as a teacher, focus on neatness and correctness in the final product but allow a lot of variation in the preparatory steps. Don't expect notes to be recopied, for instance. They are for the use of the one planning the project and do not need to be neat and beautiful. Promote the use of sticky notes that can be repositioned easily as the project takes shape. Encourage picture notes as well as word notes. Help students organize by colors and by location (piles). When possible, have students

photocopy printed material and highlight quotes and important numbers and information. Otherwise, they can mark charts and passages in books with "flags" as they collect information. Do not expect neatness and perfect spelling in the planning stages. Refine everything at the end, when all is being pulled together for presentation and allow extra time for students to do that. That time should be included in their overall planning.

9. Increase complexity if focus decreases (many careless mistakes made)

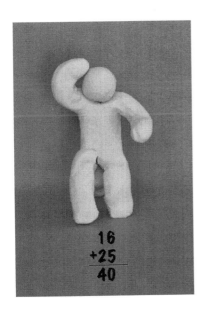 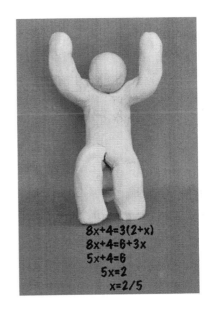

$$16$$
$$+25$$
$$40$$

$$8x+4=3(2+x)$$
$$8x+4=6+3x$$
$$5x+4=6$$
$$5x=2$$
$$x=2/5$$

Frustrated by simple computation Vs. gratified by complexity

This idea seems counterintuitive, but it is actually works. It is based on experience with experimenting with students who ran into difficulty with division (particularly long division usually taught in stepwise fashion) and fractions. Yet these same students could learn these when embedded in the more difficult area of algebra. Most of the students for whom skipping to algebra was the key to math success were visual-spatial, impatient with rote memorization, and stuck in a morass of too many steps to follow that did not make sense intuitively. When math became more complex and intriguing — more a puzzle to solve — their focus increased acutely, and you could almost see the wheels turning as they worked through the relationships involved. They were no longer stuck in a math-bog feeling they were just no good at math. Suddenly they were solving algebra problems — algebra! This was a huge boost to their self-esteem. Feeling better about themselves, their brains worked better. That's the way it is with visual-spatial learners.

A second reason to support this surprising idea emerged later. This reason was based on brain research and discovered by Linda Silverman, pioneer in research on the visual-spatial learning style. When attending a gifted conference in Illinois in 1982, she heard a presentation given by Dr. Jerre Levy, brain researcher and professor emerita at the University of Chicago. Here is what Dr. Levy had to say:

"When tasks are so easy that they fail to challenge mental capacities, communication between the two hemispheres declines and one hemisphere dominates processing with little participation from the other. Under these conditions, the attentional level is low and cognitive performance is poor. In contrast, in response to challenging tasks, the left and right hemispheres become tightly integrated into a unified brain system, which increases attentional resources and cognitive power. The right hemisphere is especially important in regulating attentional functions of both sides of the brain. Unless the right hemisphere is activated and engaged, attention is low and learning is poor."

You have probably had that experience yourself. Imagine that, in some nightmare, you had been assigned the task of counting the indentations in a ceiling tile. That is not a hard task, but it is exceedingly difficult to hold your attention to what you are doing and come up with an accurate count. Your attention, in low gear because there are no triggers to integrate your brain, keeps slipping away, and you just long for this silly job to be over. Visual-spatial learners appear to be especially vulnerable to loss of focus, perhaps because it is usually demanded for sequential tasks. An even greater problem is that basic learning strategies are quite different. There is a difference between sequential learning where mastery of each step is important to reaching a right conclusion, where understanding of everything comes together, hopefully. For a visual-spatial learner, the big picture and the gestalt of relationships is where most attention is placed. When that is grasped, then the minor parts, the details, can receive attention, but not usually before.

In her book, *Teaching Gifted Kids in Today's Classroom,* Susan Winebrenner uses this increase of focus principle when she advises teachers to challenge students: any student who can show mastery of the most difficult 10 math problems of the day does not have to do the entire assignment. Such a challenge increases focus strongly because of the possible reward. She has found that such a challenge sharpens attention while avoiding dreary repetition for those who do not need it to learn a concept. This is part of compacting the curriculum for those students who grasp what is being taught quickly. The time gained can then be used to pursue an individual project, such as reading a book of choice or researching favorite recipes of Eskimos or whatever can be done with motivation but unobtrusively. Focusing on more difficult work but less of it, is a formula that works well. Ideally, the work will involve a high degree of thinking but little writing, leaving less for a teacher to grade.

Remember that in this Tip, you are aiming to more fully engage both brain hemispheres. Let this guide you as a teacher is deciding when and with whom to complexify material. It is helpful to remember that little learning is happening when a child rushes through material and makes many errors. If this happens a lot, that student is just learning bad habits, not concepts. How infinitely better to provide a real challenge that engages the whole brain, induces real learning, and helps that student feel awesome about his or her success! The worst that can happen if you try out a more difficult level of assignment (more thinking, not more writing) is that a child continues to make careless errors. This would then indicate an area of disability to investigate and at least cast some light on the problem.

10. Be upbeat. Let good humor, appreciation, and positive emotions rule.

Have a good time teaching. Make fun of work. See yourself as the dispenser of good things to your students, like a cook preparing a feast and putting wonderfully delicious dishes on the table. That is what learning is: a fabulous feast that you have the power to set before your class. Your attitude and feelings will set the tone. The more enjoyment you have in sharing the excitement of learning, the more you find what you teach interesting and remarkable, the more enthusiastic you are about your subject and the abilities of your students to learn and grow, the more magically your classroom climate will be a buzz of involvement and success. Over and over again, research has proved the power of positive reinforcement. It really works. Each time you take pleasure in a student's advancement over where she was yesterday, each time you celebrate another student's breakthrough, each time you notice good effort and an inch gained, your approval has power. Be vocal about successes and be specific.

This is not turning yourself into an entertainment or advocating fun and games for their own sake. It is a plea for enrolling the emotional, creative, gestalt aspect of right-brain strengths in what is being learned, not just focusing on left brain mastery of details (especially through rote memory) and emphasis on lots of paper work

Encourage creative responses to assignments

There are two parts to this tip. The first one deals with providing other ways beside writing to complete an assignment. Most teachers have had experience, usually picture thinkers, for who writing is the worst kind of hard work imaginable. Many teachers pick their battles with such students, insisting on written work only when it is essential and providing construction, dramatic, or oral projects at other times. You probably already have a list of ideas for alternative projects that can substitute for or augment written projects. If not, go to Part B for such a list. This is an excellent way to bring the natural creativity, design, construction, and originality of picture thinkers into play. That leaves the opportunity to teach writing as its own subject to these students, who really require their own approach through which they can awaken their inner writer. (See our chapter on teaching writing.) It seldom makes sense to test for progress in any subject through a student's greatest area of weakness.

The second part is that creative responses may happen spontaneously when you least expect them. You felt you just explained exactly how to carry out a particular process, such as multiplying two digits where carrying is involved. Do not be surprised if some picture thinker devises his own way to do this. He may actually find a different way that works for him and provides the correct answer. The wise response to this is to allow such original strategies — provided that they work. The student needs to try that method with other similar problems. Does his idea work in all these cases? If it does, it should be celebrated. Post Henry's Rule on the wall to reward out-of-the-box thinking and encourage it in all your students. If it doesn't, Henry will know you listened to him and gave his ideas a fair try, two things which students adore in a teacher. You will be one of those teachers for whom they will give their very last ounce of effort. Such an attitude on the part of a teacher lets picture thinkers know it really is their classroom also, and they are free to try their hand at discovery.

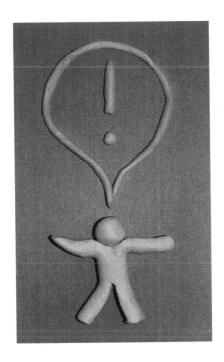

Chapter 3
Visualization: Imagine that!

One of the most exciting things that can happen for a visual-spatial learner is to learn   about visualization and the remarkable things it can do. It's like the genie in the bottle. We carry its possibilities around in our brain just waiting to be tapped.

Visualization is a spatial leaner's dream strategy. No writing or good penmanship is needed. There are no step-by step directions to remember. It can't get lost or stolen or eaten by the household dog. It is just at hand, a part of your own lively imagination.

Visualization only needs good image memory that can hold on to a picture long enough to use it. If you have the attention of a gnat, you will need to expand your attention span to make visualization work for you. There are impatient sorts of VSLs using to scanning rapidly. They watch a stream of flitting images that meld together into learning impressions. They do not pause long enough to actually see and remember details. They will need to get the hang of slowing down the stream to see a part "a few nano-seconds longer" till they can actually put that thing in their memory. They will need to experiment to find how much extra time works for each of them.

There are games to play to help you hold an image longer. With some practice, you, too, will be able to visualize. We talk about this a bit later in this chapter.

By the way, although *seeing* and *pictures* are the big attractions when visualizing, the word *image* refers to all the senses: smells, tastes, sounds, touch, movement, balance, place in space, and sense of emotions and feelings. The best visualizations use all the senses you can pack into them. You want to put all of yourself into your imaging, to be really in that scene you are going to use, seeing, listening, feeling, tasting, smelling, taking in everything that is there. Ditto for art production. Ditto for sports mastery. Be *there* and live your imaged experience. A tip: children can use their hand to help them include all their senses. Five fingers equal five senses. They can count them off without disturbing the visualization process.

This means that, as you introduce visualization, you want to teach your students to pay attention to their senses in what they visualize. Practice, over and over, being aware of sights, sounds, feelings, tastes, smells, and all the emotions that are there. Because you are working in now time, there is plenty of time to embellish the imagery.

Most spatials can let an image bloom in their mind's eye (or inner ear or wherever), fully experience it, store it, and then call it when they want. They probably are already doing it, but they think they are doing something that is not okay in school. They will probably need to be introduced to this as a legitimate learning tool. You may need to keep reminding them that it is quite okay to do this, and they will really benefit when they do. And it will also be helpful for more sequential students, who will add another tool to their toolkit.

It is important to tell your students to "look up" to retrieve images. Scowling at the floor doesn't work. Remembering how something looks involves turning your mental gaze upward to "see" it. Try it on your friends. Some may "look up" to the left and some to the right if you ask them to recall what hangs on the wall over their bed, but all will look up. Children should know that if they panic, get upset, or hunch over trying to force a memory to come, image retrieval won't work. Teach them to take a deep breath. relax, and look upward. (One more reason why a pleasant classroom climate is vital to learning for VSLs.)

Visualization is a power tool for picture thinkers. In the classroom, it will greatly benefit the picture thinkers you teach. It is also helpful to all your students, whatever their learning orientation. For auditory-sequential learners, learning to use their mental scratchpad will be more an auxiliary aid, while picture thinkers will find visualization life enhancing. They will be able to *see* how ideas work. Seeing is crucial to them, and it doesn't matter whether what they see is out there or in their heads.

Visualization is a vital educational tool to use in all classes at all grade levels. Imagery can translate all learning into lived experience just waiting to be called up and used. And for those who need to expand their working memory, it is amazing how playing visualization games can increase memory and improve focus. Visualization can relive experience, but it is more powerful than just casual memory.

Used consciously, it can enliven and enhance experience. Visualizers learn to pay attention to all their senses and to their feelings in a memory, which provides a new vitality and immediacy. Out of this come vivid, complex images for whatever you want to do with them. The new, lively memory can be restored, and when it is recalled, the images come flooding back. Again everything is vividly there for you, to use as needed.

Getting Ready to Visualize

Lead with experience. You can create your own scenario, which is fun to do. Make it a positive experience, of course, and notice that you need to provide a way to calm down and focus to begin with and a way to return to their more usual state of mind. Or you can use this imagery, a common introduction:

Lemon Action

Boys and girls, we're going to explore a talent that we all have. It's called visualizing. To get ready for this adventure, you need to prepare yourself. Take some deep quiet breaths. Breathe in, hold your breath calmly, and let it out with a little sigh. Only you can hear that sigh. Again. Breathe in hold a bit and sigh it out. Feel your energy becoming peaceful. Close your eyes and feel comfortable in your skin. Just relax, breathe, and know that something interesting is going to happen. (If some children want to keep their eyes open, that's all right. If some wiggle a bit, that's all right, too. This exercise is an invitation, not a forced march.)

Now, using either your right or left hand – you choose – realize that there is something in your hand. It is sort of round like a fat little football. You realize it is a lemon. In your imagination, look at the lemon. See how yellow it is. The skin has tiny little dents in it. There are two ends, and each end is different. Hold the lemon up to the sun and see how it shines in the light. Now hold it up to your nose. Smell that lovely lemon scent. How fresh it is! Rub the lemon against your cheek. Feel the texture of the slightly pebbly skin. Lemons are quiet; they don't make much sound. But if you tossed it lightly in the air, you could catch it in your hand with a plop! Try that, if you like. Or you can tap the rind, a little muffled sound.

It's time to take another step into lemon exploration. In your imagination, take a little knife and cut your lemon in half. You can do this easily and safely. Look at the design of the cut lemon. There is a while rim and a white center, with white spokes raying out. You can see the individual bits of lemon, almost like pulpy seeds. You can see the juice oozing out. Now put the cut lemon up to your tongue and taste that juice. Wow! It's really sour, isn't it? Let's count down from 5 to 0 and open our eyes to talk about what just happened.

Almost everyone makes a face or jumps at the sour taste of the imaginary lemon. This is a strong demonstration of how vivid imagining can be. Take a minute to let your students share what they just experienced. Make the point: there was no real lemon. Everything that just happened worked through imagery.

At this point, you will want to explain that there are two main ways we take in and organize experience. One way is through words. One way is through images. (We can also feel things with our body. We can do all three at once.) So, while we have already spent a lot of time learning to read and write and remember words, we can do many of the same things with pictures and other images. Our brains have an inner tape recorder that keeps track of our word thoughts. It also has an inner scratch pad for pictures and symbols. How exciting that we can learn to use both helpful parts of our remarkable brain!

Playing some imagination games may come next. Richard De Mille's delightful little book, *Put Your Mother on the Ceiling*, has many fun scripts to use. Such games are great for a spare moment. They do more than exercise the imagination. You will find that they raise the mood of the class. Tension eases and people feel lighter and more energized. You can make up your own little exercises. Just keep them light and fun, short and simple. Visualization is always in the here and now. Even when calling up memories, the sensations and feelings happen in the moment.

After a bit of imagination exploration, your students will be ready to use this new tool greatly to their advantage. Picture thinkers are likely to take to it like a duck to water, but almost all students will enjoy discovering what imagery can do for the. If any student greatly prefers just using words, let that happen. Individual differences need to be honored.

Classroom Use of Visualization

Let's begin with simple visual memory games. There are lots of matching card games that can be part of rainy day play stores for the classroom. Watching who excels at this kind of game is one way to sort out who is visual spatial. But equipment is not necessary. One simple game to play is "I Spy from Another Place." Just like regular "I Spy," one person announces that she is thinking of something "small and yellow" but in another place than where the group is, for example, "in the cafeteria." Players take turns guessing what this might be, scanning their memories for things that are in the cafeteria. You can prime the situation by announcing, "Tomorrow we'll play "I Spy" using the playground." Or the media center. Or the gym. That leads to more attentive looking and memorizing for the game.

Visual memory is the basis of successful visual retrieval. This can begin in the very early grades. Because you are using many visuals on the walls of your classroom, there will be several memory aids to work with. Using any visual aid you have posted, as long as it is not too complex, will do. Here are some examples with early math skills.

Let them pretend that their mind is a computer screen and design a new background for the screen. Have them draw the design they see in them imagination.

Take any word that you would like them to be able to spell. Print it in color on the chalkboard. Have your students close their eyes and print the word in their mind's eye as you call out the letters. Can they hold all the letters there at once? You may need to repeat the letters a couple of times. Call on volunteers to read the letters off in order from their mental image.

Have your young students look at the number line, focusing on the beginning: numbers 1, 2, 3, etc. Have them close their eyes and see how many numbers they can see. Check this out by asking—and having them simply raise their hands, "How many can see 1? 2? 3? 4? What is the farthest number anyone can still see? Have that student read the numbers from her head (which further reinforces the image if correct). If not correct, say them in correct order and have the class say them with you. Do this exercise again the next day and your class will discover that they can "see" more numbers. Of course, some students will already be able to count and be able to do the exercises from their own internal memory of number order. That's fine.

When most are able to see many numbers, have them play "Number Jump." The group stands with their back to the posted number line. The teacher calls out two names, say, Juan and Allie. Juan says something like, "4. Jump forward 2." Then Allie must look in her imagination, find 4, move forward two spaces and answer "6." Another first child chosen might challenge "6. Backward 3." And so it goes. Encourage children to turn around and refresh their number line image from time to time. This game can build the memory needed to do mental math story problems in class.

This same game can be played with the alphabet posting. Some children would play that game by reciting the alphabet song quickly to get to the needed letter. Those who could see the alphabet in their mind (which takes practice and works best with using sections – you could visualize cell phone groupings) would do this best. Here the teacher can ask questions like, " Does E come before or after J? Who can give the next 3 letters after E? After J? Can anyone say the alphabet backwards from W to T?" Because the alphabet is very long, you may want to work with sections at first. It's good to overlap the sections, so that all the alphabet becomes familiar visually, not just through reciting the alphabet song.

Children who may balk at writing their name for practice may enjoy "seeing" their name written in an imagined sky, seeing a magic bird or a skywriter do this, making all the loops and lines perfectly.. After a 1-minute session of such mental practice, have them write their name. Compare this to an older copy of their name. Very likely it will be improved! A skywriting plane works well for cursive writing. For printing, they may imagine a magic pencil or light saber writing on a wall or in the air. Or a can of spray paint might write the name. When they write effortlessly in their imaginations, they form a much clearer picture of what their name should actually look like. This leads to better execution of all those loops and lines and angles. Try it and you will see.

Anything that children look at can be visualized and stored in visual memory. Perhaps you have a picture of a rainbow in your room. You can teach them to remember the order of colors in the rainbow by the old mnemonic, ROY G. BIV (red, orange, yellow, green, blue, indigo, violet) or you can have them look at your picture, close their eyes and try to hold the whole picture in their memory, peek to get the order right, check their memory again, and so forth. With practice, they can see the whole bow and call off the colors in order.

All students might memorize their fire escape route, as a safety precaution. They should see themselves getting quickly into line, moving quietly along the right corridor, up or down stairs as needed, exiting the building, and assembling in a given area safely away from the building. Once this is in the memory, you can try variations: what if you are in the bathroom when the alarm rings? In a PE class, in the library? What if that exit is locked? Of course, there will be teachers to direct them, but it is also helpful for them to know the best possible routes themselves. And such flexibility of visualizing solutions to problems is excellent imaging practice.

So much for getting started. Now let's look at how visualizing can enhance learning in the subject areas.

Visualizing for Language Arts

Reading comprehension is greatly increased by making mental movies as you read. Help them do this by first listening to a guided imagery exercise, such as this one by Beverley-Colleen Galyean in her great book, *Mind Sight: Learning through Imaging:*

> <u>Ocean:</u> *Picture the ocean in front of you. Smell the salty air. Taste the salt water on your lips. Throw the water on your face. What does it feel like? Now step into the water. What does it feel like. Look around and see who or what else is around the water. Then listen for any sounds. Now dive in and go for a swim. What does this feel like?*

Let students discuss this experience. Some may want to draw pictures to go with what just happened in their imaginations. That would be great. Being immersed in this kind of experience prepares children for seeing movies as they read. Try slowing the reading down, stopping at the end of each sentence and asking, "What does that look like to you? Have them fill out details: how tall is the girl. What color is her hair? How strongly is the wind blowing?

Nanci Bell of Lindamood Bell fame has an excellent book on this called *Visualizing and Verbalizing*. Encourage readers to see the expression on the face of the Cat in the Hat as he does his mischief. What would that feel like to have to deal with a wild Cat like that? Watch Pa's fingers fly as he plays the fiddle for Laura in the Little House series. Hear the tune. Wouldn't it be fun to join the dance? Such images take you into the story you are reading, the very best way to get the most from the written word. After a passage has been read, it is productive to take some time to discuss the different images each reader has formed. All images that fit the words are okay. A wildly different image may mean reading difficulties to investigate further.

You can do a very enjoyable visualization activity with your whole class that will expand their visualization skills. Pick a short, well-written description to read aloud to them. The Little House Series abounds in such descriptions because Laura Ingalls Wilder developed this skill to make the world come alive for her blind sister, Mary. Suppose you pick the paragraph where Pa is repairing the roof. Have your students have paper and pencil at hand to be used as soon as you stop reading. They listen without drawing.. When you finish reading, say something like, "Now, you draw what you heard." Give them a few minutes to picture what they remember. Then reread the paragraph. Have them give themselves a hash mark for every part mentioned that is in their picture. You don't need to verify their scores. They are just keeping track of their own memory skills and noting how the skills improve with practice.. You could discuss what was easiest to remember and what was hardest if you like. They should keep their drawings in a folder, so they can compare over time how much better they get at seeing what they hear and being able to draw a picture of it. This will lead, in time, to picture note-taking. It also helps them pay attention to how various writers paint word pictures.

Spelling is a classic means of introducing visualization power to students. You will want to demonstrate this strategy to the whole class. Choose a willing participant and a challenging word to learn, such as "believe." Or "encyclopedia." Print the word clearly on a card. Syllables should be separated by color. Hold the card slightly above the student's line of sight. (Someone might prefer the card be slightly to the right, someone else might prefer to the left or the exact center.) Let the class know any of those positions is okay. Have the student look closely at the word, then close her eyes and see how many letters she can see with her eyes closed. Let the class know that most people need to peek at the word, often several times, until they can see all the letters with their eyes closed. When that point is reached, congratulate your student. Have her read the word aloud to you. Then, for fun, have her spell the word backwards. That will be easy to do. She will just read the letters from her imaged word. Lastly, have her go to the chalkboard and write the word from her image memory.

You will want to discuss with your students ways to deal with tricky parts of spelling words. For example, they might add their own vivid colors (fluorescent pink or vivid chartreuse) for parts of the word that are harder to remember, such as the silent "b" in *doubt* or the "ie" combination in *believe*. Letters hard to remember can also jump up and down and shout, "Remember me!" In "believe," the combination of *ieve* is tricky. You might want to imagine those letters all with polka dots or with strobe lights making them easier to remember. Once visualization spelling has been introduced, allow students who find this way works better for them to spend classroom time memorizing the image of each word rather than doing the usual writing exercises designed to help spelling memory. Students who do well with visualization spelling should not have to "practice their spelling" by writing the words a given number of times. This does not enhance spelling skills for VSLs. Getting the visual memory right in the first place is what makes the difference. Remember to explain to your class that they must "look up" to retrieve the words.

After your class has some experience in visualizing while they listen, they can learn to visualize before writing their own scenes or stories Visualization can very much enrich and enliven writing. Introduce them to the idea of looking through an imaginary window onto a scene where something is happening to write about. Playing quiet music can enhance this experience. Remind them to see, hear, feel, smell, even taste — not just see through the window. Then have them write. Remind them to include all sights, sounds, feelings, tastes, and smells. The results are usually quite an improvement over previous written work.

Work with your students to remember and reenter a memory to write about. First, go through the step of calm breathing and total focus on just the memory. It is important to enter deeply into experience. Now have them put themselves in the memory and pay attention to all they see, hear, feel, taste, smell, their feelings, their thoughts, and anything else that seems important. Quietly, and perhaps with soft music playing in the background, have them open their eyes and begin to write. The quality of the writing will be much better, with rich details and much more lively language than usual.

Some children may want to make a quick thumbnail sketch of the scene, which becomes a focus point as they write. Otherwise they are likely to forget a thought as their fingers strive to keep up with their ideas. This is especially helpful for children whose thoughts move very quickly. Other children will be deeply focused in their experience and won't need the sketch.

Even when writing about something that is being made up, it is helpful to spend time letting the scene play out in your imagination. You can "see" characters interacting before you start to write. This is like writing a movie script while watching the movie unfold. Watch the characters in the story come together. See what happens and what they say. Then quickly write about what you saw. These methods are likely to produce writing that is fresh and lively and interesting. Freeze Framing the parts of the "movie," a more advanced writing procedure, will probably be necessary.

Visualization can improve punctuation. Visualize some writing where all the sentences have a period at the end of each sentence. All the periods are big and round and a favorite color. As you watch, all the periods jump up and down and wave "Hi! We're glad you didn't forget us." Children can look at what they have written, image periods at the ends of sentences, and then actually put them there. Now, they can check that each sentence begins with a capital letter. See them, then write them in. This is fun to do with a crayon or marker. That way, the periods and capital letters really stand out in the writing and are more memorable. There might be another color that is used for making question marks. And another for those exciting exclamation marks!

Students studying speech and debate need to keep key points in their heads and may keep a mental web or a checklist of talking points in their mind's eye view, just like excellent poker or bridge players. These might be points they have written out first, or for some reluctant writers, there may be symbols that represent the points to make. Whatever works!

Visualizing for Math

Math facts can become silly, unforgettable pictures. One example is seeing a picture of a foot walking oh! so carefully on a dozen eggs sitting on top of a ruler where each egg occupies one inch. (1 foot = 12 inches). This builds on the earlier knowledge that 12 equals one dozen. This is ridiculous but memorable. Go to the web site www.multiplication.com for more ideas about making math facts memorable.

Read a math story problem to your students. As they listen, have them draw a picture of the problem as they understand it. Have several student display their pictures and explain how they think the problem is to be worked out. Discuss which pictures best present the problem and why. Then, using either paper and pencil or mental math, have them solve the problem. Visual-spatial students often excel in mental math because slower writing interferes with their math thinking. Try another session in which they make a picture in their mind to explain the problem as they understand it. Can they make this into a mental movie in which the needed operations take place? There are students for whom this method works very well. Others may prefer paper and pencil. Each should be allowed their preference.

You can visualize parts of a math word problem, turning the numbers into amounts of something you like, like scoops of ice cream, or footballs, or M and M's. You can see the parts of the problem acted out like a cartoon. Watching the cartoon helps to clarify how to solve the problem.

Imagine you have four friends over and you are playing a card game. Your deck of cards contains 52 cards. To divide them equally, you deal them out, one to each person including yourself. The first round of dealing uses 5 cards. The next will take five more, making 10 cards dealt. How long will it be before all the cards are dealt? How many cards with each person have? Are any cards left over?

Imagine you have a stash of M&Ms (50 to be exact) and 6 friends to divide them among, including yourself, of course. This is just another problem like the one above. Children man need to peek to write down the number of M&Ms involved in each deal (which is okay) or they may be able to keep all the numbers in their head. Such visualizations reinforce the idea that dividing is like dealing rounds. You take out equal groups until you can't do it any more. You might have some cards or M&Ms left over.

Playing with fraction tiles or other manipulatives can help students see how many eights equal one half, for instance. After working with the actual tiles, students can visualize placing the smaller fractions on top of the larger ones, like one-half. They will get familiar with what fits (those with a common denominator) and what fractions are incompatible. Seeing that two sixths fit into the space of one third is helpful, meaningful information. Realizing that no number of fifths will fit into one-third is also meaningful.

Decimals may be more understandable with the following visualization:

Place a numeral 1 on the chalk board with a decimal to its right. Have the class imagine taking another number 1 and cutting it into 10 pieces, each of which are yellow. Mentally put the pile of yellow pieces in the place to the right of the decimal. Use yellow chalk to mark that space. Next, have them take a yellow number bit and chop *it* into 10 pieces. All these pieces are orange. Mark the orange space with orange chalk. Add nine more piles of orange number bits the same size (there will be 100) and squeeze them into the next space on the line to the right. In your imagination, see each of these orange bits chopped into 10 very tiny purple bits. They get crammed into the space to the right., marked woth purple chalk. Although its hard to see, there will be 1000 of them. (The imagination can do things like this easily.)

Now write a decimal number, such as 1.328 or one and three hundred twenty-eight thousandths. 1 will be black, 3 will be yellow, 2 will be orange, and 8 will be purple. The previous visualization showed how much progressively smaller a bit each number to the right represents. Color coding makes bits in each decimal place stand out. It also gives a sense of just what a number like 1.328 stands for.

Many math texts have illustrations that lend themselves to visualization: pie charts, graphs, equations, the angles within a triangle, why the area of a triangle is half that of a corresponding rectangle, etc. There are translucent math materials that can be used with graphs and other background materials on overhead projectors, so that students can follow the operations like a little movie. Such practices lead to still further eyes closed visualization exercises.

Visualizing for Social Studies

Simulation games enhance the imagination and bring history to life. They can be computer-based or acted out in the classroom. Visualization is a vital part of that enactment. This is the natural way little children play. As they grow older, their ability for acting out their imagination fades, but it can be reinvigorated. As history, or yesterday's headlines are dramatized, learners are much more actively engaged. Learning takes hold and is remembered. Drama is a close cousin of visualizing. Acting something out greatly enhances learning. Dramatization aids visualization and visualization aids the creation of scenes and role playing. Both make learning a real experience.

History becomes easy to remember when you add labels of details you want to remember to pictures of important happenings. These may be already in your textbook or in a movie you are showing that you can pause and comment on. A voiceover you "hear" or a banner pulled through the sky you "see" can remind you of why this scene is important. You can open your mental dictionary and pull out that word you want to spell (if you put it there in the first place). You can see the letters in the hard part of that word in your favorite vivid fluorescent color. All you do then is simply copy the word from your mind. Don't forget to look up! You can have an important biology term jump up and down and wave to you: "Don't forget me!" as you scan your mental *Grey's Anatomy*. The more you use color, action, cartoon characters, and humor in your images, the better they will work. Visualization is great fun!!!

It will be fun for you and your students to learn to experiment with what you can see and move around in your mind. We live in an age of TV, video games, movies, and cell phones with screens. Everyone is used to electronic screen techniques. We know about fade-ins and fade-outs, split screens, voiceovers, wide-angel vistas, zooming in to focus on and enlarge details. We are all visually literate. There is no limit now to what can be imagined and how it can be treated when visualizing. And this field of visual learning has only just begun to flourish!

For example, you can use images moving through a split screen to compare the tribal ways of Iroquois and Sioux cultures (or the country mouse versus the city mouse). You can zoom-in to a mental picture of the Grand Canyon to watch the burros picking their way along a narrow canyon trail against the layered rock sides and "see" the color of the rocks or the weeds growing in the trail. It's possible to zoom that text diagram in last week's lesson to see the details in the lower left-hand corner (if they were in your mind when you studied the diagram).

Visualization can greatly enhance important moments in history, as when Balboa actually caught sight of the Pacific Ocean after struggling across the isthmus that strings together two continents.. What did that feel like? How important was that moment? What actually happened then? We don't know, but we can imagine. Close your eyes and imagine what that looked, sounded, smelled, felt, tasted like. Was Balboa's heart thumping? How was he feeling? What was going through his mind? What were his men saying in the background? In creating such a visualization, you *become* Balboa, making this great discovery, unforgettably. Out of such visualization might come a dramatic sketch about this important historic moment.

Visualizing for Science

You can put yourself in the middle of what you are learning and gain a close-up perspective of what you are studying, say, in science. You can be the atom moving sluggishly or expansively depending on the state of the matter of which you are a part. You can see you and all your fellow atoms locked into rigid place as ice, see yourselves floating free from one another as heat melts the ice and produces water, and see yourselves floating off into space, each a distant part of water vapor. Feeling that difference makes the concept concerning states of matter more understandable and more memorable.

Science students can better understand laws of physics by taking time to imagine themselves as substances affected by the law. For example, they can "be" magnets and experience in their imagination how opposite poles attract and like poles repel. "Experiencing" the power of magnetic forces at play produces a grasp of magnetism that reading and talking alone cannot supply.

Science students can visualize themselves carrying out experiments and discover what parts they understand and where there are glitches in their knowledge. This can lead to better preparedness as they study those points of uncertainty to see better what can be expected to happen then. Such preparedness can make the actual experiment more meaningful and the results, whether expected or unexpected, more significant.

Visualizing for Sports

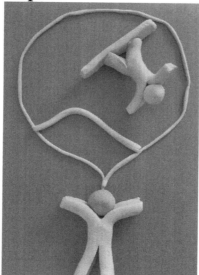

The sports field has long known the power of visualization. There have been experiments in which one group of basketball players practiced free throws, another group visualized standing at that line and watching the balls sink through the basket, and still another heard a lecture about how to improve their ball-tossing. The surprising thing this is that the visualizers did almost as well as those who spent time practicing. That's quite remarkable. Imaging is very close to actual doing. Books about the "Inner Game of Golf" and the "Inner Art of Skiing" began to spring up after this experiment and now abound. They tell us how "seeing" yourself succeeding is the royal road to actual skill improvement.

In sports, you can focus and visualize yourself making a basket, sinking that put, catching the spiraling football, hitting the baseball to an exact target area, or having perfect balance on the balance beam. Visualization enhances performance, as research has shown, spawning books like *The Inner Game of Golf*, to name one of a spate.

Visualizing for the Arts

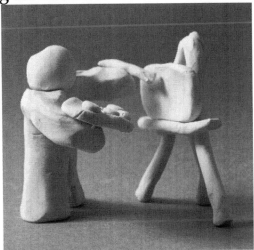

Music class students can imagine themselves singing on key and producing a gorgeous choral effect. Their actual singing will improve, if only because they are each focusing together (practicing inside) before they began to sing. They will be surprised at how well this "trick" works. They can also learn to "hear" notes in music they are reading with their "inner ear." Remember, all the senses are involved in visualization, not just sight.

You can "see" a picture in your mind before you paint it. Your final picture will probably be different from what you imagined, but it will be enriched by your mind's eye view with all its vivid detail and sensuousness.

Drama students can learn to "see" the play unfolding as they read it and learn their parts. Seeing the whole play unrolling in their head as they rehearse helps trigger the complex memory of movement, placement, and lines they need to call up the whole scene as they move and speak. The director has a special visualization job. She or he needs to be able to see the whole play unfolding as well as "zoom in" to the lines and movement of individual actors, while keeping open an esthetic sense of how it all flows together..

Still Other Aspects of Visualization

Visualization can do even more than build strong memory. It can enhance understanding, provide new ways of looking at things, and manage or transform feelings!

Imagination can be used to gain new perspectives. It can aid such things as learning to draw a scene from either a bird's eye or worm's eye view. This also helps in realizing that things can be seen from a variety of points of view. Such exercises stretch the imagination and exercise flexibility. These activities would not be graded because they are gutsy experiments in expanding consciousness. However, the process of even attempting them makes for perspective-stretching discussion.

Visualizing a new perspective can go a step further to imagining yourself in someone else's shoes. What do things look like from this new angle (literally and figuratively)? "In Their Shoes" becomes a way to gain the feelings and experience (all imagined) of what someone else may be going through. This can be used with characters in stories or with people in the news. It can expand empathy and understanding of other's positions and feelings.

Visualization can even be used to change mood. Help your students to build their own "wonderful place to be" in their imaginations. Return to this exercise, "My Favorite Place in the World," from time to time, adding new details or changing what is there in any way they choose. They should practice this from time to time, paying special attention to the sounds, the feeling in the air, the smells and changing colors, any music or food or animals that might be there, until their special place becomes vivid and wonderful and a real mental refuge for them.

The next step is to teach your students that they can take a "mini-vacation" by closing their eyes, taking a deep breath, and mentally putting themselves in this special place. Once they can call up this scene speedily, the mini-vacation becomes a teacher's friend. Suppose your class has just come in from recess, hot and bothered by some quarrel or contention. It is wonderfully soothing to take time out, breathe deeply and encourage everyone (including you) to enjoy a mini-vacation before starting the next lesson. Or, after everyone has worked hard taking a test, it's great to relax and take a mini-vacation as a reward.

Visualization can help children be more self-aware. Many advisors teach children to imagine a dial with numbers, say, from 1 to 10. This dial can be set in the imagination to the number that best represents how a child feels at the time, with 1 being "Really Bad" and low energy, and 10 being "Really Great" and full of pep and vigor. Once students get used to this image, they readily can learn to set the dial to represent their present mood. This provides language to talk about how they feel. "I'm not happy today. I'm at 3." "I finished all my work early. I'm at 9!" They can also experiment with discovering that they can move their dials one or two numbers up or down on their dials, and their feelings will follow. This surprising happening occurs more times than anyone would suspect, further proof of the power of imagination.

Visualization can also help children make better choices in the way they behave. They can be taught to stop when they feel themselves getting angry or reckless. What is the number on their dial? Stop a minute and breathe. Then, urge them to look in their mind to see what they think the outcome of their action will be. Is this what they really want? They can keep imaging other actions until they see themselves doing what makes them feel best. Of course, making wise choices takes a lot of work and practice and will work better for some children than others. Yet once a child actually experiences making a good choice this way, the experience is quite powerful and memorable. Visualizing can empower for good.

These suggestions only open the door of possibilities a small crack. There are so many ways visualization can enhance your students' understanding of what you are teaching. Go ahead and create your own visualizations, and find out what works best for you. There are only some main considerations to keep in mind:

Most of the time, all students will choose to participate in visualizing. If some students are not comfortable doing this, let them use more traditional methods of reinforcing their learning.

Always make the visualizations positive. Scary pictures or frightening ideas are not what you want your students to be inviting into their mental storage units.

Remind your students that not everybody sees pictures in response to visualizing. Some will hear sounds or words. Some will have gut feelings about what they are learning. Such images work in their own way and can be just as effective as images that are seen.

Chapter 4
Whole Word Reading

Reading Problems of Picture Thinkers

Picture thinkers love stories. They adore being read to, love movies and video games, and have the vivid imaginations that make the most of fantasy and sci fi genres. They do have some quirks and foibles that run counter to more traditional ways of teaching reading and with the usual ways of analysis of contents and organization of reading products.

There can be bumps in several places along the royal road to reading. There can be problems with phonics-based reading instruction from the very first with some spatials who have trouble with the isolation of sound bits and their use. Whole words or syllables will work better for them.

Some spatials try to turn the sequential act of reading (one word after another) into getting a sense of the whole by trying to read a whole paragraph or page at once. They rapidly span for keywords and make an intuitive guess at the contents, which is sometimes right and sometimes wrong.

Reading is often image-based, and there can be trouble reading many words for which there are no images, such as "the," "for," "while," "until," — most of the Dolch word list, actually. Such words may elude the memory of spatial readers, so that they need to be learned and relearned. Using a larger, more memorable unit works better.

Some picture thinkers have vivid imaginations that take them off the page. The images that accompany their reading (which can be quite proficient) take them off into fantasies engendered by phrases they are reading. They are off into somewhere else without realizing what has happened. This is a real difficulty and hard to aid.

Because spatials are tuned in to relationships and the connections that arise among the many parts of a seamless whole, they often have problems with finding the main idea or with any analysis that requires looking at different levels of reasoning. Theirs is a democratic point of view that sees all as equal, except for exotic bits that interest or fascinate. Outlining or organizing thoughts can be a challenge. However, they are great at seeing connections and finding many solutions to a problem.

Subtle differences between words of similar meaning may elude VSLs. For some artistic and image-oriented readers, words are labels for pictures. There isn't much need for synonyms or attention to precise gradations of meaning. On the other hand, their language is often striking and poetic, and they respond to poetry deeply.

The ideas they take away from reading may be impressionistic and simplistic. They may need help in *seeing* how details enrich. Reading the fine print or deciphering convoluted and complex sentences may need special attention, although their love of solving mysteries can motivate them to do so well once their attention is turned to this challenge.

The Phonics Road Bump

Picture thinkers have natural strengths that should lead easily to reading. Their keen awareness of shapes and visual details produces the kind of visual discernment that supports early reading. Many of them do love to play with those interesting shapes that are letters and numbers. "Look," they will say, "there's a Y in those tree twigs. I see an X and there's an A too!" "I can bite these Cheerios into a C and a U!" "Look at the W's in that bridge!" They are hugely excited that their life is full of symbols.

Many picture thinkers are wonderful readers. Often they begin at an early age to read signs and symbols — MacDonald's arches, STOP signs, Toys R Us. They know the different makes of cars and their logos. They follow along when someone reads a favorite story and pick up words like "hop" and "pop" and "cat" and "hat." They push to learn more words, asking constantly, "What does this say?" Others start with whatever gets them into the computer and turns on their favorite games. Once in, they learn a few words that they need to play. They soon learn a few more words and enough strategies to help them get to the next level. That kick-starts the process for them.

Still other picture thinkers memorize favorite books and progress from there to recognizing words and phrases in the stories, and soon, before anyone realizes what has happened, they are reading new easy readers on their own. If the excitement of reading hooks them, they take off, intensely scrutinizing new words, deciphering many, skipping others, and reading whatever appeals to them, usually something well illustrated. All these assertive readers have by-passed the phonics road to reading and are happily absorbing new words before they enter school. Although they often bypass words, they can tick off the major happenings in the story to whoever queries them. They vividly "see" the stories in their imaginations as they read. Like the best readers, they read for meaning and anticipate what will happen next, using context and pictures and their own sense of the story to guess/read onward. Reading, for them, has just happened.

Yet picture thinkers may have reading problems that do not affect sequential beginning readers. Let's look at why that is.

Picture thinkers tend to recognize shapes in any orientation (an upside-down K is still a K to them). They are just as likely to write a 2 backwards as forwards (as are most young children). Many love to write their whole name backwards or upside-down. It's still their name. It's harder for them than for sequentials to get that letters have one right way to go. This can lead to problems with letters like b, d, p, and q and with numbers like 6 and 9 that when flipped or reversed have new meaning. That's a detriment, especially if eyes are moving erratically here and there rather than smoothly along a line of print.

That is one possible stumbling block to reading for visual-spatial learners. They tend to make many reversals and inversions in their reading and writing and to persist in doing this after other children have stopped. These children may sometimes be seen as having a vision-related form of dyslexia (although, today most dyslexia theorists see dyslexia as more related to language and hearing).

Still, many picture thinkers go to school eager to learn to read or read better. Dutifully, they work to learn all the letters of the alphabet and their "sounds." Although memorizing separate little bits of information is harder for picture thinkers, a surprising number do manage to do this. They start to read primers. Primers are written with a special vocabulary of sight words already learned and a few new phonetically regular small words. Some linguistically controlled primers use only words easy to sound out. Most are three letters long and result in sentences like, "The fat cat sat on the mat." Most picture thinkers do well with such short words, although they are not thrilled with the stories.

Picture thinkers even learn phonics rules, such as the "Silent-e Rule," in words like "hope" and "love." But when reading books move on to words with blended consonants and longer words, like "whisker" or "strange," a group of picture thinkers hit the blending wall. "Sounding out" no longer works for them. Let's see why.

Picture thinking spatials are gestalt learners who work best whole-to-part. Details come later. What they are being taught in the "sounding out" method is to pay close attention to tiny sound bits (really small details) and to build up words from these bits of sound. Phonemes — or the sounds of each individual letter or letter cluster — are too tiny for picture thinkers to identify, let alone work with naturally. So, what they do in the "sounding out" process is turn each bit into some kind of whole by adding "uh" or some such sound to make a usable unit. This creates a series of unrecognizable sounds. "Fuh-lah-auh-tuh. What is fuh-lah-auh-tuh?" Guh-uh-eh-sss? What is that! It is foreign to them. After plowing through three or four such puzzles in a sentence, they have no idea what they just read. Picture thinkers don't lack skills or motivation or intelligence. They really want to learn how to read. But, somehow, they can't slide those phonemes together quickly to make a word that makes sense. They would get immediately that "flat" rhymes with "hat" or even that "guess" rhymes with "mess." And if told to look at the word and see "This is what 'flat' looks like. This is what 'guess' looks like," the strength of their visual memory would help input the word into their mental computers for future use.

This misfortune does not happen to all spatials. For a lucky group, teaching reading "phonics-first" is fine. Only some picture thinkers get stuck, but they are really stuck. The harder they try, the less confidence they have. As the problem continues, they begin to believe they are stupid. Remember, picture thinkers ride their emotions as they learn, and their brains shut down when flooded with negative feelings. If they see other children "getting" reading while they flounder, their confidence plummets.

The general situation for non-blenders is that, although they can decode some words, it is a hit-or-miss process. Confronted by an unfamiliar word, they tend to get the sound of the first letter, look at a nearby picture if one is luckily there, and guess some word that begins with that sound. Sometimes their guess is lucky, and it looks as if they know what they are doing. More often their guess is off the mark.

Because blending seems to be such a sticking point, more phonics instruction is usually brought to bear. This seems to make sense — improving an area of weakness — and sometimes it does work. There are intensive phonemic awareness programs that can provide breakthroughs. Sometimes, intense multimodal instruction, such as the Lindamood Bell program, Orton Gillingham, or specialized programs that focus on hearing the sounds correctly — such as Earobics or Fast ForWord — (to name some of the most familiar) provide the boost that does the trick. For picture thinkers, some of the best of these phonemic awareness programs look at the patterns of words. They use variously-shaped colored blocks to represent the sound patterns, and these visual patterns do make more sense to picture thinkers, who are great with patterns.

Sadly, there are some picture thinkers for whom these programs, although excellent, yield only frustration. Lots and lots of practice with lots and lots of details.Insipid stories with no emotional punch. Frustration. These children may work really hard and only win through to plodding, stilted reading that rings no bells. Remember, spatials thrive on emotional highs, get gestalts, play with patterns, look for significance and meaning. But these programs focus on their weaknesses and, unfortunately, offer the reverse of what works naturally for these children. Why not go with their strengths instead?

Strengths That Work

What are those strengths? Spatials learn in wholes or by getting the Big Picture. They remember what they see. They do not follow step-by-step directions or sequences well but try things out, often inventing their own methods. They are active learners who loves games, strategies, and humor. They learn through aha! moments, *see* what they know and remember that etched-in-the-brain image forever. Even when their own way flops, they usually do better taking the "bugs" out of it than by trying to follow an instructor's stepwise plan. They need some method that uses their innate qualities — something magical.

These children can read whole words and have already done so. Their brains are activated by meaning, fun, imagination, and emotions. They are more sensitive than average, feel strongly, are easily hurt or discouraged, and want positive feedback and support. They are good pattern finders who thrive on discovery and the aha! experience. They can learn to read any word — like the name of a friend — that has meaning for them. They can probably read it upside-down and backwards as well.

There is a method, not well known, that has been around since the 1960's, but which has been submerged due to research that strongly favors teaching reading through phonics. That research is persuasive. The problem is that there are some picture thinkers for whom it works poorly. These children can benefit from being taught by the Whole Word reading method. Not the same as Whole Language Reading, and originally called by its inventor, "Organic Reading," Whole Word Reading uses spatial strengths of visual memory, emotional connection, and pattern recognition. It truly is more organic and natural for them.

Sylvia's Way: Organic Reading

Whole Word Reading builds on the work of New Zealander Sylvia Ashton-Warner, who, back in post-WWII days, found herself in a crowded pre-fab classroom teaching mostly Maori five-year-olds to read. The bland stories in the usual primers were a total turn off to these children whose lives were completely different. Unaware of the visual-spatial model but determined to engage their young minds, Sylvia resorted to her own intuitive method: to excite and empower them, she decided to let them each chose their own words they wanted to learn. This unorthodox method she called "*organic reading*." Her Key Vocabulary, the first set of reading words for these children, came directly out of their own lives and feelings.

Sylvia's engaging books, *Spinster* and *Teacher*, tell the ups and downs of her experiment, which, becoming successful, began to catch on and be imitated. These books give vivid accounts of how a rebel successfully turned non-sequential minds onto reading.

Sylvia began every day asking each child what new word she or he wanted to learn and, without censorship, printing it on a sturdy card. If a child wanted "blood" or "kiss" or "knife," she printed the word out. Most words obtained in this way, she found, were "one-look words," integrated at once. While she was engaged one-to-one with each child, the others were busy reading their own sets of words from earlier days and illustrating and writing stories that went with their words. As they finished, they read their stories aloud to each other. They also shared their new words with each other. This made for a lively and sometimes chaotic classroom, but it was one in which these more right-brained children were successful.

Another of Sylvia's activities was to have each child read aloud words from his or her word card stash each day. She listened and quietly removed any words not remembered. To hold on to their words, the children needed to truly learn them. The words they could keep became theirs and were an informal tally of the progress they were making. Children also tended to learn their neighbor's words as they overheard and saw words they might like for themselves.

As their pile of words grew, the children's stories became more elaborate. Even if a child stuck to writing only a few words or just one sentence, all were gaining a sense of mastery of words from their own life, words they really wanted to be able to read and write. Many children began to write many words, and could put those words together to tell exciting stories. They were invested in getting better and better, always building on a solid reading vocabulary that originated with their interests and what they thought was important. Sylvia's children learned to read and write and did it at a level above other comparable five-year old non-sequential students.

Sylvia, whose days were filled with drama and who kept a bottle of rum in her desk drawer, was not a model for every teacher, but she was a hero in the remedial reading classes I took at the University of Vermont in the 70's. There, Dr. Lyman Hunt, Jr. was championing "organic" methods of reaching struggling readers and engaging Dr. Jean Chall, a strong proponent of phonics-based reading, in national debate. Dr. Blanch (Betty) Royce, working under Dr. Hunt, seconded his philosophy. A reading specialist who had run into major frustration trying to teach children in the Virgin Islands to read, Betty had found that the usual phonics methods did not work. "Organic reading" methods had much more success. Betty Royce ran an Action Center for reading teachers that focused on creating games and manipulatives to enhance whole word methodology. She supported a child-friendly learning atmosphere — rocking chairs, snug reading corners, games and active discovery enhancement, focus on success, discarding what did not work, and repeated searches for what did work. The exemplary teachers of reading she had her students visit were calm and positive and nurturing and warm. Much of what she promoted was not readily quantifiable. Nor do I think her methods work for or are needed by every reader. But I think that for some children, including those spatial learners with blending problems, they are the secret of natural success.

From Organic Reading to Whole Word Reading

As our Denver center that supports gifted children began to work more with visual-spatial learners through the pioneering efforts of Dr. Linda Silverman and her deep interest in spatial children, a light came on for me. Some reading difficulties of visual-spatial students had a familiar ring, and I realized that activities and theory learned at the University of Vermont fit these particular problems. I recognized that the Maori children and the children of the Virgin Islands were probably visual-spatial learners. This was why they needed different reading methods. There are other populations, such as Native Americans, who are more attuned to space than to time and that learn the visual-spatial way. However, the visual-spatial learning orientation is by no means reserved to indigenous populations. There also are many creative gifted learners who have this orientation, and the growth of incidence of spatials among us is on the rise. Children across the intellectual spectrum may be visual-spatial. There is a global phenomenon in falling verbal scores on the SATs while quantitative scores hold fast, an indicator of a movement toward nonverbal (spatial) reasoning skills worldwide. Fields testing for identifying visual-spatial students revealed consistently as many as one-third of students to be spatial. Further analysis shows that, actually, there are more students that really benefit from visual-spatial teaching methods than from strictly auditory-sequential methods. Most classroom, however, remain strongly sequential in teaching that occurs there. Educators have not yet realized that this switch is going on.

Sound-blending problems made sense in terms of known visual-spatial traits. Strong in recognizing patterns and grasping the whole of something, although poor in sequencing, spatial learners who, although obviously bright, were struggling with reading seemed good candidates for trying Sylvia's methodology. Why wouldn't organic reading work better for them? They too, learned best when their emotions were engaged, were brilliant with pattern recognition, and had powerful visual memories. Although no one I knew in the reading field was using Sylvia's reading method (the reading wars having been won by the phonics side), it seemed time to revive it, at least for these spatial children. What about using wholes to teach reading to these children — whole words, that is?

I began to suggest Whole Word reading to clients, even though there were no working models other than Sylvia's books and some brief suggestions I handed out. The feedback was positive; the Whole Word approach worked. Letters and calls from surprised and pleased parents testified to that. Dr. Linda Silverman included a section on "Whole Word Reading Instruction" in her comprehensive book on visual-spatial learners, *Upside-Down Brilliance: The Visual-Spatial Learner.* An article on the method, called "Wholes and Patterns," appeared in the Spring, 2003 *Gifted Education Communicator,* a quarterly published by the California Association for the Gifted (CAG). As the ideas of Whole Word Reading reached a larger readership, feedback continued to be positive. Grateful parents wrote that their children had experienced breakthroughs. While Whole Word Reading may not be needed for every picture thinker, it is worth considering. .

Why does it work? Let's begin with emotion. Picture thinkers do best when they feel positive about themselves and their surroundings. Good feelings really help their learning to soar. Whole Word learning engages positive feelings. It uses words that children themselves choose, words that they care about learning. It uses games and game-like activities to engage them with their words. It asks them to be creative and have fun. It is not competitive or belittling in any way but rather uses jokes, silly sentences, and such strengths as visual memory to engage them fully in using what they have learned, providing drill and practice unobtrusively. Right away, they get to know words they want to be able to read and use, and everything they do adds to their sense of owning new knowledge and succeeding. They relax and enjoy it all, which puts them in the very best position to learn.

When — after a while — phonics rules are introduced, they can take this new aspect in stride because phonics is taught in a way that engages their strong pattern recognition. This is analytic phonics, comparing how differences in a beginning or ending or middle letter of a word changes it in predictable ways. It is far easier for them than sequencing separate letters into a new word. They can see how letter addition and subtraction changes a word they already know, because they are working with the whole word, and that makes sense to them.

Getting Started with Whole Word Reading

The environment in which Whole Word Reading takes place needs to be friendly, comfortable, and supportive. The process should be fun and exciting. Remember, good moods speed picture thinkers' learning. Whole Word reading is different enough from the usual reading lessons that it is best taught to its own group.

Each child in the group will need a tub or container in which to keep a stash of words, ongoing word projects, and drawing materials. Each child's words can be stored in a special "Treasure Box" decorated by that child or on a large snap ring that holds cards with a hole punched in each. The tub should be large enough to hold ongoing projects in various stages of completion. Picture Dictionaries, child-created picture books, magazines to cut up, crayons, markers, and other art materials should be readily available to the group. Because handing out new words to learn is an individual task, there need to be ongoing word-involved tasks to occupy the rest of the group while the teacher is writing out words for each child.

The group should meet in a section of the room where visuals abound. Posters on the wall showing color words, classmates' names with photos, words for emotions (these charts showing faces with varied expressions — each with its descriptive word are common in teachers' helper stores), useful actions (play, sing, hide, run, fall, eat, etc.) are useful for supplying words the children may want to use. Picture dictionaries are a great resource. Have several of these on hand. Also helpful are dramatic pictures illustrating useful small words that are hard to remember by themselves but easier to remember in silly or striking phrases. Some examples are "from the dragon's mouth," "under the silver moon," "where is the ghost hiding?" or "that pest!" More about this strategy of sneaking Dolch words into reading vocabularies later.

You might begin each session by reading a short story and talking about it with the group. Pick an interesting word from the story, such as *heffalump* and offer it to all who want to learn it. These cards can be prepared ahead of time. Of course, children do not have to take the word if they do not want it because choice is important in Whole Word reading. But one common word can get things going, giving children a word to copy, illustrate, and memorize. Each child also may be given 1 to 4 more words that they want to learn. You will soon sense how many words each child learns easily. Print the words on cards and give them to the child. You want to get across the idea that exciting, important, big words are the best to add. Some children may need help to think of a word that is important to them. Be relaxed and patient. It will take some children a while to understand these words are really theirs!

While this one-to-one process proceeds, children may be drawing pictures to go with a favorite word, copying and decorating their words, decorating their Treasure Box, or arranging their words in a way they like and might like to read quietly to a friend. You will find that many children listen to the words that someone else gets and are quite interested in them. Some children will learn several new words "on the side" in this way.

What happens after a child receives her words? She is to trace the letters with her finger and then write the word on paper large enough to draw a picture that goes with the word—her choice. Children who don't draw well can choose pictures to cut out from magazines. When the picture is finished, word cards are stored in Treasure Boxes and the pictures go in a folder. Alternatively, the children might write the words, one word on a page, in journals, illustrating each word.

The next day, tip out the words from the boxes face up into a circular "pool" in the middle of the group. Each child gets to go fishing and fish out his or her word(s), If there are words that are unclaimed, quietly discard them. They were not memorable. Have a child choose a new power word instead. Children should also be free to copy a friend's word if it appeals to them.

By the end of the week, each child should have 4-9 sight words to play with, enough to begin some word games. The more words in each box (or ring), the greater variety of games are possible. Games are drills disguised as enjoyable activities, which are fun in themselves and also fun because no one is ever "put on the spot" to demonstrate what they know. You want to create success from the first, using a child's emotional ties to her words to provide the magic of rapid learning. Here are some ideas for activities. They are not definitive but are given to show some possibilities. You will soon find yourself creating new games as you see what works best with your group.

A good game is to have photos of all group members on a poster, with each child's name attached on a card (try artist's putty, or velcro.) Take down the cards for the Whole Word group and scramble them. Allow the children as a group to put back all the names. This is always successful, because each child will already know his own name! This game can be played often, until each child can put up all the names in the group, or even all the names in the whole class.

This same game can be played to introduce animal names. This is a sneaky way to build sight vocabularies of words children may not have chosen but would like to know. Just be sure to choose interesting and favorite animals. Don't try a chart of Dolch Words, those bland "little" not-memorable words. That would be too discouraging. (Remember, those most wanted can be included in a memorable phrase with a striking illustration and posted on the wall.) Other subjects, like foods, sports, holidays, coins, or car models can be posted from time to time.

Here is a good game to get things going after each child has his or her words. Put a sentence on the board with two

important parts missing, such as "How astonishing that
_____ found _____in his lunch sack!" Read this to the
group and invite children to add two words from their pack.
The words should be displayed as the silly sentence is read by
the child. Who can make the funniest sentence?

Here is another. Each child chooses two or three words
to use in their own silly sentence. For example, "The **rhino** ate
purple **watermelon**." That child's words, "rhino" and
"watermelon" should be visible as she says her sentence. Go
from child to child and listen to their sentences. Go ahead and
laugh with them. This is intended to be fun and funny.

Later on, have a sorting day. Each child takes 12 or
more cards out and sorts the words into category piles. Each
must be able to tell what kind of thing is in each pile, such as
Toys, Things I like, Scary Stuff, My Favorites, etc. You will
need to get this started using one child's chosen words and
showing how to set up categories as an example. Invite
several different ways to sort out a given set of words. This
builds flexibility in thinking. Children share what they have
sorted and explain why words go in each pile. Again, this
exposes each child to others' words and also exercises their
thinking skills.

Play "What Am I?" Pin a child's word on his back
without letting him know what it is. Whisper to all the other
children what the word is unless it is a word that all know.
The child who is It tries to guess the word. He can ask yes or
no questions only. This builds thinking skills and strategies.

All of these games benefit from being played many
times. They become patterns into which words can be
inserted, the beginning of reading and writing sentences.
When the teacher is working with one child, the rest of the
group can be creating "books" out of pages of pictures they
have drawn with one-word captions (or short phrases for

those who can manage this).

Spend some time just talking about words. Talk about soft, silky words like "lullaby" or "murmuring," bold words like "stampede" and "strike," interesting words like "radar" or "willow-the-wisp" or "Rumplestiltskin, and silly words like "higgledy-piggledy." This activity is a wonderful vocabulary builder and helps children pay attention to words themselves. It is fun to do often. Make a word tree out of a branch. Stand it up on your desk or a table and hang special words from each branch. Or put new-found words in a golden frame on a bulletin board.

Two or three children can sort through their stash of words for words that go together unusually to create a mood. What would "flimsy caterpillars" feel like? How about "fierce kittens"? or " pearls," "peacocks," and "petunias"? This is the beginning of writing and appreciating poetry. You might want to read some poetry with remarkable words to them and encourage creating word associations to post on the wall.

You get the idea. Any situation in which interesting or alluring or powerful words come into play can supply material for Whole Word reading.

Playing with Word Patterns: Analytic Phonics
At, mat, splat, flat, splattering

When your spatial reading group has collected a large number of sight words they comfortably know, it is time for Part 2 of the program — time to introduce analytic phonics. Analytic phonics works in a different way from the usual sequencing of letter-sound relations ("sounding out" words). It teaches understanding of sound-symbol relationships through comparison and analysis of whole words, affixes, and root words. For example, we look at how changing the first letter of a word changes it to a new word, as how *get* becomes *net* or *sister* becomes *blister*. This kind of analysis has always been a part of understanding phonics. We just introduce it in the second stage of learning to read rather than the first. Because the students have learned a large number of sight words, they now have many recognizable words to work with. Rather than sequence tiny sounds to make a word, they get to work with patterns and their transformation.

There are many ways to begin this. Take your pick:

One way is to use any suitable word that the class is looking at in one of their activities. It should be a word in a "rhyming family." Say, you are using the word *black*.

Explain that you are going to play the Letter Magic game with them. Write the word on the board and erase the first letter. "Abracadabra! Now you have a new word, *lack*. Erase that first letter. It is not a word anymore! But, by Letter Magic you are going to make a new word. What if you put a "p" in front? What is the new word? What if you add *age* to the end? What if you add *s* to the end of that? Wow! Isn't this exciting! You now have "packages." Close your eyes and see the word, "packages." Can you still see all the letters? Go ahead and peek again if you need to till you can hold all the letters in your mind's eye — that eye you see with when your eyes are closed. Who can spell "packages" backward? (For more on visualization spelling techniques, see page X.)

There are endless versions of this game. One is to start with a tiny word on the board, say "ad." Make a long list of "ad's" underneath. Challenge your readers to come up and make a new word by adding another letter or two in front. When they do create a word, circle it. When it's a bogus word, X it out and discuss why. It might be a hononym of a real word that is spelled differently — something you will be learning about later. For now, stick with words that fit the pattern. You are building a vocabulary of common word families in the English language.

Another way begins with spelling. It also uses word families but is more advanced. It builds words out from a small beginning word, like "hog." Easy transformations here are log, frog, jog, etc. — but you can also build words like blog, eggnog, jogging, slogging, pollywog, and even transmogrofy for Calvin and Hobbs fans. You are not really teaching spelling here but playing a game that helps your young readers see how word parts can be building blocks. You are showing them that word patterns can be transformed at the beginning, at the end, or even in the middle, as when "splash" becomes "splish, splosh!"

There is even a spelling program, called AVKO Sequential Spelling that uses the building block principle and does teach spelling. If you can get your hands on it, you can use it as the bones of your Magic Word Game project and not have to think up words for the game. They are all set out for you in seven levels.

Encourage your children to try extending any of their words. This is a chance to teach some common suffixes (-s, -ing, -er, -ly) and prefixes (un-, down-, over-, super-). Talk about how the root word, "cool" changes when you put "un" or "super" in front. What about "down cool" Is that a word? No, but "cool down" is useful.

You have probably grasped by now that Whole Word reading has quite a different tone to it. You are not presenting your group with information that they must memorize and be tested on. That is much more a sequential way of teaching. It is a way that does not work well for picture thinkers who won't remember isolated words (unless they love them!) The Whole Word way includes no comparisons between children and no direct asking "What does this word say?" which puts a child on the spot and blasts the learning process. It may not feel like teaching at all, but it is actually a wonderful way of reaching children's minds that helps each child feel able and empowered.

Whole Word reading has a much lighter touch, is fun, includes creativity and choice, and builds on pattern recognition as a basis for decoding new words. Your main task is to create a climate of fun that helps each child pile success on success. Each child is building a large set of words and word patterns that are building blocks of reading. They will move on to decoding unfamiliar words just like sequential children, but have taken a detour around the "sounding out" method.

By the way, the entire class, sequential and spatial alike, can be included in analytic phonics work. It is an alternative way of addressing word attack skills and works in ways that enliven and integrate the classroom.

Ongoing whole word work
Each day you meet with the Whole Word group and give each child new words they want to learn while the rest are illustrating their words or creating "books" of drawings with 2 to 5 word captions that are stapled together. You play some word games with them, encourage them to read words or play with word groups they choose with one or three friends, to browse through picture dictionaries, and to write sentences that use some of their best words.

I hear you saying, "But how can they write captions or sentences when they don't know all the words to put in?" Teach them refer to the many words posted with their pictures on the wall. They can leave a space where the word should go. (Some may be able to hold that place with the first letter of the word. Then, you have a time when children quietly line up and ask for the word they need. Quickly print it on a sticky note and hand it over. Children then copy their words in their sentences and post the sticky on the inside cover of their folders for stories that is in their tubs. Next time a child needs a word, she should check that inside cover to see if the word is already there.

It's easy to see that we are at a crossroads here. To write a whole sentence, the children will need to know how to spell many common words, like "the," "of," and "under." Now what? You have already trained them to leave a hole in their writing where the word they need can go. They have gotten used to your giving them individual words they need on stickies. Now they are ready for the next step.

It's time to add those useful Dolch words to the sight vocabulary. Which ones? There are so many of them! One of the easiest ways is simply to keep chalk in hand and write the Dolch word asked for on the board. Have the child who asked look carefully at the word, say it, close eyes and spell it, and then write it down wherever they need to use it. Add other words as asked for. If the same word is asked, put a dot after the word. If there are 3-5 dots after a word, that is a word worth teaching. Yes, you actually get to teach some words of your choice to this group. Here's how to keep that enjoyable.

Suppose the word to teach is *said*, which is likely. Add a cartoon picture of someone talking to your printed word. Show what is said in a bubble, just they way they do in cartoons. In this case you can do comic strip conversations. Readers quickly learn phrases like "Charlie Brown said," and "Lucy said" when written with the word *said* in color beside the posted comic strip. Leave this up for reference for budding writers. A class project can be to write a silly conversation of two sentences between two people (or two animals, or two articles of clothing, etc.). This gives lots of practice writing and reading *said*. And makes for lots of giggles, which aid learning.

Because you are focusing on good ideas children have and what they **can** do, you are not expecting perfect finished products here. Some students may need to simply **say** what was said, rather than write it. Others may be able to write most of the words but have to leave some holes (which they fill in orally when they read aloud). You, with your handy post-it pad, can hand them the correct word so they can copy it in. Encourage sharing of words to copy.

"Said" sentences can be taken one step farther. Correctly copied silly conversations can be duplicated to become play scripts. Duos can present short skits reading from the scripts and using distinctive voices. (Give them a bit of time to plan how they will act their script out. Taken still farther, working with "said" becomes a teachable moment when comic strip balloons, lines in a play, and quotation marks can be compared. Quotation marks then make sense: They only go around the words you would put in the cartoon balloon!

Make lists of words that are community property (needed by everyone) and post them. You can set up a Word Wizard routine, perhaps setting a beautiful big feather (or a laser pointer) near the board with its word lists. Anyone who is not sure of a word there can point to it with the feather, a signal for the child who knows the word (the Word Wizard this time) to come up and read it quietly to the inquirer.

Place illustrations of words-with-many-dots around the room where children can easily see them. Again, use that strategy of putting each of these bland words into a memorable phrase. For example, "on" becomes "**on** top of spaghetti" with a cartoon character sitting on top of a plate of spaghetti—easily put together from magazine clippings. ""For" might be "**for** Pete's sake!" "From" can become "running **from** the Cookie Monster." You can tackle a featured word every few days and then arrange these in a row above the chalkboard for easy reference. For "the," you might have a contest. See who can write the longest sentence with the most "the's" in it. You will probably get something like, "The cat saw the frog eat the fly on the day I got the chicken pox." Obviously, these budding authors will need help spelling many words. Again, it's the sticky pad to the rescue.

Sticky pads are a picture-teacher's best friend. This truism is why teachers should always wear clothes with pockets, so that pens and sticky pads are at hand. Jotting a needed word for a child becomes an almost unconscious habit. You whip out your trusty sticky pad, print the word on the sticky, and stick it in front of the child to be copied.

Back in blend land
Suppose you are working with the children on a word family like:

> hip
> ship
> chip
> rip
> lip
> skip
> trip
> triple
> cripple

Slipping into the analytic way of teaching phonics (because knowledge of phonics is needed for reading) and you realize you are back in Blend Land, where all the trouble started. How are you going to introduce blends in a way that your picture thinkers won't be trying to say chuh-huh-ih-puh instead of "chip?'

It's time to bring out Tongue Twisters to help teach letter sound blends. These should be fun and memorable. For the "ch" sound, you might introduce, "Choose the cheery chimp with the Cheetos." Can they say the tongue twister twice fast? Your aim is that they memorize the twister, so each one you or your class create should be funny and fun. Post tongue twisters with the blend letters in color.

You can have fun making up your own Tongue Twisters. Create them based on class need. What blends are they struggling with? Here are a few to get you started:

Blue blimps make me blink.
Fling your flip-flops on the floor.
Please play on Planet Pluto.
Phone the photos to the phantom.
Frisky frogs are my friends.
Greta grows great green grapes.
(a more extensive later)

You are likely to discover that some of your picture-thinkers are actually beginning to read, needing help with a few words just like any other reader. They have been using their word stash, learning friends' words, and getting the idea that words often fit families. They realize that if you know a member of the family, you can figure out their cousins and aunties. These "catching on" readers will be able to read easy readers, like *One Fish, Two Fish* or *Hop on Pop*. Encourage them to do so and encourage them to write silly books of their own, singly or in small groups, each writing a page for their group book. They can draw their own pictures or solicit other students to be artists for them. Such projects lead to a kind of choral reading of the book to the reading group when the book is complete. Video tape the performance, so they can see themselves later and others can enjoy their book also. These videos show next year's students what the possibilities are.

It's easy to see how this progresses: engage the emotions, encourage the use of special words in games that aid the memory process, add a lot of creativity and fun to building sentences and small books, play Word Magic to focus on analytic phonics and word parts that fit families and teach hard-to remember words in memorable phrases that are posted for easy reference.

When, and only when, your picture-thinkers have learned many sight words, are able to play the Word Magic game well, and your walls are covered with resource words and phrases, you may begin to read stories with them as a group. Use overhead transparencies, so that all see the story together. Use a pointer to casually underline each word or phrase as you come to it. Invite all the children in the group to read quietly aloud together, as in Impress Reading. There will almost always be someone who knows what a new word is. If no one figures out the word, that is a teachable moment. Does the word fit any word family? Is it part of a phrase on the wall? You can read ahead to see if context helps. As a last resort, simply tell them the word, "It's *unicorn*. That's what *unicorn* looks like. Close your eyes for three seconds and *see* it.* This is a habit to build. Always say, when giving a word. "Look and see what *skedaddle* looks like. Close your eyes now and see it."

When the short story is done, go back and read it once more. The group is likely to be able to read all the words when they can support each other. Take time to talk about what happened in the story. What part was best? Why? You can dramatize the story by having each child take a role and pantomime actions as the story is read again, if this is needed. (If you have more students than parts, they can tag-team the parts.) Offer a copy of the story to all who want to take it home and read it to their astonished parents. (Remember, this is on your computer and easy to print out.) Keep it all low pressure.

The Whole Word group is now reading much like your other reading groups. More story material can be presented to them for group work, but you also want to let them continue to write and illustrate their own stories and books. Practice figuring out new words with them as a group. What word family helps here? Let them help each other with words. Play with more word patterns and add more affixes. Let them read each other's "books."

Not everyone in the Whole Word group will proceed at the same pace. Some will catch on to decoding and surge forward. Hooray for them! Others, who are slower to learn new words, need to take more time. Don't push any child to take on more than she can assimilate. It's better to stick with one or two word families than to take on too many. Introduce some stories with controlled vocabulary. They can read about how "Stan ran to dance with Fran. Man! He was a fancy dancer." There are many readers available with controlled vocabulary available for your use. You may want to play more visual memory games. As some children begin to read more independently, they can be reading books of their choice, while you work individually with others. By the way, early "book reports" need be no more than 1-3 illustrations to show what happened for these picture-savvy picture thinkers. Encourage captions for these drawings. They make a great basis for an oral report on a book someone really liked.

One problem you may have with Whole Word reading is that the other reading groups will be jealous of all the fun. Do let them join in by doing their own projects, writing "books," creating word poetry, or thinking up their own tongue twisters. All the Whole Word reading projects can only add to and reinforce what you are already teaching other groups. All teachers know that some of the best learning happens when groups eavesdrop on what other groups are doing. There is something about tangential learning that makes it stick! As other children take up some of the projects you have introduced to your Whole Word group, you will find your whole classroom has become more enthusiastic and involved in reading. Picture thinkers do add verve to a classroom.

Creative reading – another road bump

Do you remember that scanning for significance is a strength for visual-spatial learners? This trait may affect their reading also. Many spatials, especially those who taught themselves to read at an early age and who pour over catalogs at home or browse through *National Geographics*, are not reading every word. They scan the page just as they scan any room they are in or everything they can see anywhere they are. They are actually trying to read the page all at once, rather than read rows of words sequentially. Some become quite good at absorbing key words, especially if those words make pictures in their minds. The pictures come together quickly to form a story that they take away, feeling that they have "read" what was there to be read. This could be called "creative reading."

Jeff Freed, the co-author of *Right-Brained Children in a Left-Brained World,* and a marvelous tutor of visual-spatial learners, makes use of this tendency to scan. If he is working with such a child, he has them go ahead and scan a paragraph or short page or writing and then tell him what they just learned. Usually they will be able to produce several bits of information. Then he has them go back and re-scan the passage and tell everything new that they just learned. A third, or even a fourth scan will yield still more information. Jeff's method has some resemblance to the Evelyn Wood speed reading technique, where an entire page is viewed in a swoop that covers the page. Following the swoop, key words are jotted down in a pattern of connected lines easy to scan when reviewing. Jeff's method is useful. It makes use of a natural tendency and takes it farther to develop a way of absorbing a lot of information. It is especially good for reading to learn situations and reading in subject areas looking for the answers to questions.

Jeff did not stop with multiple scans. He also had those he tutored pick a paragraph to prepare for reading aloud, mastering every word until it was possible to read fluidly and with expression. In this way, he combined a way of reading that was natural to many picture thinkers but also provided word attack and oral reading skills. The ratio of scanning (a lot) to polished reading aloud (a little) works well. All this is a far cry from the usual way children are taught to read, but it can be useful, especially for older readers who have been reading this way for a while and find it very hard to read word by word. Scanning strength must not be confused with the kind of word jumping and loss of place that happens when children have visual tracking difficulties. They need to be seen by a professional who will do vision therapy with them.
Because scanners find the big picture first and only fill in details later, they may glide right over important details, such as the word, "not." A way to help them search through "the fine print," is to give them, from time to time, complex sentences (and later, paragraphs) that require careful reading just like the lines of a contract. Ask them to orally paraphrase what they just read in simple language. For example, " She was not completely unhappy that her father failed to be on time this once," translates to "She was happy her father was late." Complex math word problems also serve this purpose. If you have practiced drawing diagrams to sort out such problems, this is a parallel kind of practice, clarifying the reading of tricky sentences and promoting good math reasoning at the same time.

Do insist that your readers make movies in their head as they read, seeing what is being said. Research shows that such visualization helps comprehension. Take time to ask questions when a group reads a story together. What kind of road does the little red hen walk down to call on her friends for help? What does her voice sound like? What expressions do you see on her friends' faces as they refuse to help? Nanci Bell has written an excellent book, *Visualizing and Verbalizing*, which details how to build visualizing strength. Making movies as you read can also help you check that your reading makes sense. If the movie gets fuzzy or turns black, go back and check what you read. Insisting on things making sense is a major aid to good reading.

The Words-You-Can't *See* Road Bump
Words in clay: the Davis way with Crystal Punch

Another reading method valuable to picture thinkers was created by Ron Davis, author of *The Gift of Dyslexia* and creator of the Davis® Dyslexia Correction Program. Go to www.dyslexia.com for details about this excellent plan.

Ron Davis developed a program specifically for that group of picture thinkers whose dyslexia interferes with reading. His method engages their natural ability—their gift—which is to "see something new from all sides" at once—helpful for hunter-gatherers telling food from foe but not helpful for reading print. If you look at print from all sides trying to figure what a letter is, the fact that **p, q, b,** and **d** have exactly the same shape is not helpful. A **w** and an **m** can be confused. An **n** looks like a short-stemmed **h**. And so on. Ron Davis insightfully discovered a method to look at print from a fixed orientation rather than that all-around perspective so natural for picture-thinking dyslexics. He tamed their experience of print.

A second Davis insight is that picture thinkers easily become disoriented when they are confused. Decoding words they cannot image is confusing. In the Davis lexicon, these are called "trigger words." Picture thinkers generally create pictures in their mind when they read. Words like "car," "sock," "fence," and "horse" all conjure up a picture. However, enough trigger words like "the" and "was" and "from" lead to confusion. Yet such words are the basic connecting words of our language. There is even a list of most of them, called the Dolch list. Most Dolch words cannot be pictured and so are trigger words that cause confusion and then disorientation Enough patches of confusion, and the thought process is interrupted, stopped, or disjointed. This creates huge frustration.

The Davis Method helps the picture thinker build a visual/kinesthetic dictionary of these "non-image words" to create an easily remembered and felt meaning for each word. Clay is used to construct words that have a personal connection to the reader and become part of remembered experience. Actually, creating a visual dictionary from clay can help all learners who are stumbling a bit with reading. It is an easy, enjoyable approach that has been done in quite a few classrooms. Davis's book, *The Gift of Dyslexia*, goes through the procedure step-by-step. Here we will give a brief summary.

A clay area can be set up in a corner of the classroom. A soft, pliable, oil-based clay (that will not dry out) is used to create 3D pictures and words. Choose a confusing word — almost always a "little" word, such as *how*. Whatever time needed is taken to help the child understand what that word means. The dictionary is consulted. The word is used playfully in a sentence or in several sentences. The child should be able to state the word's meaning in a way that shows real understanding, not just parroting what she has been told.

Ron Davis teaches: There are three parts to understanding a word:

- o The way it looks: the very letters that make up the word and their order.
- o The way it sounds: how we pronounce the word aloud.
- o What the word means: what it means in this particular sentence.
- o

Take the word *any*. It's a little, hard-to-remember word, and it can be confusing. Here's an example. "I want a banana but I don't have any." My dictionary says there are four different meanings of the word *any*, but in this exchange, it means "even one" or "the possibility of one." Of all the bananas there are in the world, I don't have one. *Any* is like a place-holder for the possibility of having a banana. Once the reader can describe what the idea of *any* is, she creates the word in clay. Something about the feel and sight of making the letters and putting them in the right order makes them more memorable. It is also helpful to anchor the idea of the word by adding a clay "self-figure" (a little figure that represents the reader) connected in some way to the word *any*. Perhaps the reader will sculpt herself with a tray of pencils: "*Any* pencil will do to write with." Or she might make a countertop in a candy store with three candies on it. "*Any* candy will make me happy." It's up to her.

The next time the reader comes across the word *any*, the experience of any pencil or any candy will rise up out of her memory. There will be no confusion about it. Or, if there is, it's back to the drawing board to make a better clay image that clarifies the meaning.

To help you as a teacher understand how trigger words cause confusion, consider this typical story a student of yours might be reading. Remember, almost any word can be a trigger word—a word that triggers disorientation. Here is some story text:

"A family of four lived out on the plains. They had lived there for seven years and had a herd of cows and a few horses that roamed the land."

"A family of four" is probably imagined as 2 adults and 2 children and probably understood as human beings. It might, however, be confusing to some. "*Plains*" might confuse a reader who didn't know that term, but if known, it produces a clear image. "*Herd*" might confuse a child not used to watching Western movies and would be thought of as a "something" of cows. *"Few"* might be a trigger word for some. *"Roamed"* might be a trigger word. However, talking about these words is probably enough to make sense of them. Having a child draw a picture of the scene can clear up any misunderstanding. The visualization exercise of reading a description and then having children draw the scene they imagined can be used to clear up any misunderstandings and could lead to a brief discussion of how many cows in a herd and how many horses would "a few" be.

When reading a story line, most picture-thinkers can quickly deduce what the story is about, especially if it is illustrated. But when reading a sentence in isolation, as on a test or a list of directions, the opportunity to misread or not understand increases. The small connecting words: and, in, the, where, over, on, etc. then become critical to understanding what was just read. Clay work is an excellent resource to deal with recurring misunderstood words. It resolves these problems.

Making Bland Words into Wholes

One other way to deal with the bland words for which there are no images (those Dolch words, for example) is to create a memorable phrase that includes the word. Then a strong visual memory can see the little, forgettable word as part of a stunning whole.

For example, the word "for" could be part of an exclamation, "**For** crying out loud!" This goes with a memorable face contorted with emotion, both angry and tearful. Tears should be flowing in exaggerated fashion. The word "for" should be printed in shocking pink or some other memorable color. Or you could use the Three Musketeers' slogan: "All **for** one and one **for** all!"

Here are some other examples:

The bland word "from" can be included in the phrase, "Escape **from** Doom." The picture this caption accompanies needs to be dark and scary, with figures shown fleeing for their lives. Again, "from" should stand out visually from the rest of the caption.

The bland word "with" might be part of "the best breakfast— frogs' legs **with** hot sauce. "The" might be embedded in "I am **the** best snowboarder in the world!"

Think about "my" as being part of "**My** broccoli is greener than **your** broccoli!" You can squeeze in two bland words for the price of one picture. The sillier or stranger the phrases the better they will be remembered.

You get the idea. Word posters should be made for the bland words that are causing the most problems with your readers.

The Road Bump of Summarizing: Finding Main Points
Table with the legs

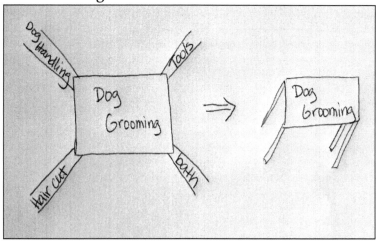

Speaking of movies, a picture thinker lives the experience of being in the movie as he watches. It becomes part of his personal memory. If you ask him what the movie was about, he can replay it for you scene by scene, probably reconstructing the dialogue and even dialect. But ask him to summarize what happened in a neat little paragraph, and he is stumped. Spatials need help with the art of summarizing.

Summarizing a movie is a big job. It's better to start with a paragraph and that classic job of finding the main idea in the paragraph. Even that will be hard. VSLs do not naturally hierarchize or categorize. They notoriously have difficulty with multiple choice tests because all choices present interesting ideas to them. What to do about this?

Crystal has developed the strategy of using a cutout paper table and its legs to illustrate the idea of the main idea in a paragraph. The main idea is the top of the table and the supporting sentences are the legs holding up the top. There are several ways to use this idea. You could have an overhead drawing of a table or a small model of a table and practice with the class analyzing a paragraph to find the main sentence. Various sentences from a cut-up paragraph can be tried as the main one that belongs on the table top. Do the other sentences—which become the legs— really support this idea? Class discussion can help develop the ability to judge. You might create worksheets with a table and four legs to cut out and fold into a table. Also include a five-sentence paragraph. The sentences are to be cut apart and glued or draped in place. Again there can be a class discussion about what it means to support an idea versus being the main idea. The cut and paste aspects of this exercise appeal to spatial learners. At first it might be wise to work with paragraphs that have four supportive sentences. Later you can work with paragraphs that have three or five or even six supportive sentences. There *are* tables with different numbers of legs.

Writing headlines that tell what happened in a few words is another way of approaching summarizing. The headline will be another way of looking at the main idea. In this case, you are creating the main idea. It stands out in black letters at the top of the story, a brief, telegraphic way of telling what it was all about. Students can bring in news stories with headlines. You can make a teaching bulletin board by separating the headlines on one side of the board and positing the stories on the other side. Use numbers one side and letters on the other to designate each item. Students try their hand at putting headlines with the right story. A flip-top pocket hides the answers, so each one can check correct answers.

Graphic organizers, usually used for organizing thoughts before writing, can also be used for summarizing a paragraph, an informational article, or even a book. Can you find a pattern among the graphic organizers that fits what you just read? Is this something with a main part and five subparts like your hand and its five fingers? Is it like a tree with a main-idea trunk and several branches (and twigs on the branches). Is this like a ladder or a set of steps that takes you from here to there? Is it like a file of dominoes where something happens that makes another thing happen, that, in turn, makes still another thing happen? If you were to make your own graphic organizer for this story, what would the main pattern be?

Of course, all these strategies can be used for sequential students as well as spatial learners. They may be more needed by the spatials, though.

More about Reading with Visual-Spatial Learners

Let's jump ahead down the reading road. There is still more to learn about some glitches—at least for teachers—that are fairly common in the reading of visual-spatial learners.

The first is that picture thinkers are much more comfortable with reading silently to themselves (where they often do a good job of comprehending what they read, which can be checked out through questioning them about the contents). They do well with computer reading programs that involve reading passages or little stories and then answering comprehension questions afterward. Most really can get the gist of what they are reading. However, when asked to read aloud, they may stumble over words; be dysfluent in their reading with long pauses, omitted words, or poor phrasing; or just balk at beginning what is embarrassing for them.

Why should this be? It seems as mysterious as picture thinkers' notorious struggle with handwriting. There seems to be an innate awkwardness when spatial learners try to coordinate certain activities, such as thinking and handwriting or thinking and reading aloud. Perhaps future researchers will be able to give us answers about this. For now, we can only observe that some situations that work perfectly for left-brained learners are hard for right-brained picture thinkers. Simply know that if you call on them to read aloud without prior preparation, you are asking them to perform in an area of weakness. On the other hand, based on the winning idea of working from strength, it makes sense to engage picture thinkers in silent reading comprehension programs, whether a boxed set of cards is used or a computer software disk.

Helping them read aloud more fluently requires some strategizing. One idea is to involve them in drama. Acting is a wonderful way to make reading come alive. I am not talking about full-fledged plays with many actors and lots of lines to memorize but rather brief scenes or skits with a short bit of dialog, something conducive to "hamming it up." Encourage broad gestures and silly voices, the more dramatic the better. If a picture thinker is having fun, he can often accomplish things he simply can't bring off at all when doing so exposes his weaknesses. Being a dramatic star is quite another situation.

Brief dramatic scenes can be used to develop children's evaluation skills. Ask a group of two or three to act out "the scariest part of the story," "the part where a problem is solved," or "the part that surprised you most." Give them a brief five minutes to plan their action and then — on with the show! The more youngsters do this kind of thing, the better they get at it, gaining more fluency without realizing it.

Choral reading is another activity where reading voices can be improved. This works well during a poetry reading unit. Many poems cry to be read aloud. By quickly designating which students are to read which lines or stanzas, including solo and group parts, the poem becomes a production. Encourage your students to listen to the effects of the varied voices. They may have ideas for alternate interpretations and effects. Tape record their work and play it back for their satisfaction and critiques.

Tongue Twisters for Better Blending

Picture thinkers who are having trouble blending letter sounds to make recognizable words are helped by tongue twister play. A silly tongue twister can model the sound for a blend that will stick in the memory. Since pattern recognition is a strength, they are using a strength (pattern recognition) to deal with an area of weakness (blending sounds), and that's a good thing.

The sillier the tongue twisters are, the more they will be remembered. You and your class can have fun making up your own twisters for troublesome blends, but here are some ideas to get you started. Hopefully, most blends are included here:

I can blog blindfolded on my blackberry.
Brenda broke the bride's breadstick.
Cheering chimps choose Cheetos.
Clams clap for clever clowns.
Crazy crocodiles crunch crayolas.
I dream of droopy drippy dragons.
Fling your flip-flops at the flood.
Frisky frogs make friends freely.
Gleaming glaciers make me glad.
Greta grows great green grapes.
The knight had a knife in his knapsack.
Phone the photos to the phantom.
Please play on Planet Pluto.
Prod the prince with a prune.
That scamp has scads of scars.
I screech and scream at scribbles.
Shove the sheep in the shed, Sheila!
Skeletons skid when they skate.
The sled slid down the slick slippery slope.
Smell the smoke and smothering smog.
Snakes snack on snips and snails.
Spots and specks sparkle in space.
Spray sprinkles on the spruce.
Squeeze the squirmy squealing squid.
Stack your stuff on the stairs, Stuart.
Strew string along the stream as you stroll.
I think thick thorny thoughts.
Trust trees to try new tricks.
Twist twenty twigs into twine.
Whale is whistling and whining.

Visualizing to Spell

The needed entry skill for success here is good visual memory. If you are teaching a picture thinker whose images flit too fast to be "seen," then visual memory needs a boost. Games to develop visual memory, such as "Concentration," are in order.

However, many children need only to take "a few nano-seconds longer" to look at a word (or a writing web, a teaching poster, a model, or other visual information source) to be able to call it up in detail later. Remembering is an individual matter, and it's good to encourage pupils to try different lengths of attention to discover their own best time to insure memory.

Basically, here's how Visualization Spelling works:

The child needs a copy of the word to be learned well-printed on a card (a 5 X 8″ card folded lengthwise is a good size). Word models should not be student-generated, but they can be computer generated, using a 49 or 72 point font. You want a good model to visualize. Print each syllable in a different color. Alternate black and red, for example.
The student holds the word to be learned about 9 inches in front of her eyes and slightly above the line of sight. It's fine if she prefers a word held more to the left or right. Placement of the word should feel comfortable.

The child scrutinizes the word, taking in all the letters. Then she closes her eyes to see how many letters she can see in her mind's eye. If they are not all there, she will need to look at the word again. And again, until all letters are seen with eyes closed.

At this point, there are several choices. The student may simply spell the word out loud to a partner, reading from his mental image. He may write the word from memory. He may choose to spell the word out loud backwards — which is fun to do and an impressive "parlor trick." Backward spelling should always be followed, though, by spelling the word again forward.

If a child knows he tends to forget, he should do the nano-second thing, or take extra time to over-remember the word. Another trick for strengthening memory is to walk away from the Spelling Center, walk around the room once or twice, and then come back to the Center and still see the word again with eyes closed. Check accuracy by spelling it to a friend or writing it from memory.

There are other possibilities. After correctly spelling the word, the child might count to 50 by 5's and then retrieve the word from memory. Or she might count backwards from 20.

Any interrupter can be used to help fix that word image strongly in the mind.

There are wonderful advantages of Visualization Spelling. If the word ends trickily in "-ance," the **a** can be emphasized by making it a standout color, like shocking pink, !" All sorts of things are possible in the imagination. Then you would never end the word in -ence.

You can picture a hammer nailing "i before e" or the other way round if needed. That **p** in "pneumatic" can vibrate and be a foot tall. The **eau** in "beautiful" can be a trio that does a song and dance. The more silly and outrageous your image is, the more that word will be engraved in memory. All this is quite fun to do and provides a feeling of mastery over the dread tricky spelling word.

Always remember to LOOK UP to retrieve visualized words.

Chapter 5
Math for picture thinkers

Many of the best mathematicians are visual-spatial. Because picture thinkers' main strength is their ability to see and find patterns, they have the potential to be outstanding in mat. After all, math is all about patterns and relationships — recognizing systems and using them to build new structures using the language of numbers. Picture thinkers should shine at math and some of them do. Many love to think about and play with numbers before they start school. However, because picture thinkers have real difficulty retaining facts outside of a framework or big picture view, *memorizing isolated math facts is often a disaster for them.* That is one reason why many picture thinkers fall apart when asked to do timed math fact tests. They may also be poor at computation because they never memorized the facts and instead count on their fingers, either real or imagined in their mind's eye. Often they miscount. They often make other careless mistakes and think they are really poor at math.

Picture thinkers who stumble around with computation often come to hate math. Yet, this is a shame because they grasp math *concepts* readily, and their methods of problem solving are usually on target. Picture thinkers understand intuitively how math works. If their self-esteem can hold out till they reach the level of geometry, algebra, trigonometry, and calculus — the advanced math stage — they suddenly discover that they are math wizards, *seeing* how the systems work.

Likely problem math areas for picture thinkers are:

It's hard to memorize math facts, especially the multiplication facts. These remain unconnected and slip out of memory if not part of some sort of web.

Written drill work doesn't work for them for two reasons: a) Awkward writing interferes with thinking and slows down drill work. Even when facts are remembered, there may be written mistakes. b) Picture thinkers think in pictures and store facts as images in memory. Written drill does not improve these images. In fact, the frustration of writing them out tends to erode the memory of them.

- Following steps is unnatural for them, especially if presented verbally. Many algorithms are stepwise. Long division is a nightmare!

- Rules (someone else's thinking) can be hard to follow unless also visually presented.

- Keeping track of numerators and denominators in fraction work is confusing. This is a problem for all kinds of learners.

- Factoring can be slow, unless factors are *seen*.

Unless new concepts are encoded in meaningful symbols or pictures, they may be very hard to manipulate and use in real problem solving.

How can picture thinkers be helped to learn math through their areas of strength? What techniques really work for them? This chapter looks at some ideas and suggestions that are winners.

Working from Right Brain Strength

Let's look again at some outstanding picture thinker characteristics. These learners are strong in recognizing relationships and patterns and often scan their surroundings for them. They like to explore and invent, often coming up with original ways to do something, meaning that they are strong in the kinds of thinking that are useful in problem solving. Their feelings are interwoven with their thinking, and vice versa, so engaging their feelings is important. They remember what they see and experience but tend to forget what they hear. Putting all this together, a different approach to math that uses these strengths makes sense for picture thinkers.

First of all, Singapore math, which uses many pictures—especially in the early years—often substituting pictures for words, works really well for picture thinkers. This is a well-researched, continually updated program. If your school is already using this program, you are well on the way to picture thinker success. However, for other schools, we have some good math suggestions.

One aspect of early math that works well for picture thinkers is the fact that the curriculum in preschool, kindergarten, and primary grades is usually generous with pictures, games, and manipulatives, all of which are really helpful for picture thinkers. Teachers use real objects to count and are good at teaching one-to-one correspondence by counting all sorts of things. Adding and subtracting are often tied to real life situations and are done with pictures or tokens. Lots of materials are self-correcting, so there is instant feedback. As long as there is not too much writing involved, picture thinkers readily learn early math concepts.

However, learning math through writing can be a problem. Many picture thinkers balk at any kind of writing. They resist written worksheets because maneuvering a pencil to create numbers and letters is such a struggle. They also resist written math because the slow, awkward act of writing interferes with their math thinking, which tends to be rapid. When writing, they lose their "thinking place," make careless errors, and seem to have a problem coordinating hands and mind.

On the other hand, picture thinkers love mental math and excel at long mental math stories: "Suppose you had two M and M's, but your friend came along and you gave her one and then there was a packet of eight M and M's in your lunch box, but you ate five and a squirrel stole 2 when you weren't looking. How many would you have left?" This process will be interrupted and possibly stopped cold if picture thinkers have to write down the numbers along the way. Further, having to write explanations of each step of problem solving — a practice of some math programs meant to insure understanding — will truly interfere with their math reasoning skills. It's quite hard for them to hold to their train of thought and write at the same time.

It makes sense for these children to practice writing improvement separately and to demonstrate math understanding in other than written ways. In general, it's best to require no more than minimal writing when teaching math to picture thinkers. So sprinkle math sessions with mental math minutes and look for non-worksheet ways to practice math for your picture thinkers. Ideas will be provided below.

Those Pesky Math Facts!

Let's look at the problem of memorizing math facts. It's true that math facts need to be accessible. One way to do this is to make a calculator available and proceed to build strength in setting up and solving problems. Another way is to establish math facts as patterns that can be seen. This may be a new idea, but it is a basic strategy when working with picture thinkers, who may forget what they hear but remember what they see. The strategy is that addition and subtraction facts are first *seen* as patterns that are visually memorable, then reinforced through math games, and finally made quickly available through computer software and other kinds of games. (While most computer math games reward fast recall of facts already learned and do not use patterning as part of the game itself, they are still far superior to math fact worksheets for picture thinkers.)

So, how to get over the hump of memorizing math facts? The key words for picture thinkers are *patterns* and *games.* Here's an example of using patterns when learning math facts.

Start with a target number, like 5. Invite your class to come up with all the ways they can think of to make the number 5 (or its equivalent). Put these on an overhead transparency. Do they see any pattern here? Then switch to a transparency that looks like this:

5 + 0	0+1+1+1+1+1
4 + 1	1+1+1+1+1
3 + 2	1+1+1+2
2 + 3	1+1+3
1 + 4	
0 + 5	

Somehow, seeing all these combinations and relating them to the overall number they add up to works better than just memorizing 3 + 2 = 5. It is both more game-like and more exploratory. Seeing a system and remembering its parts works better for picture thinkers. They need to have visible systems available to consider and take in. Be sure to copy the transparency and post it for easy reference.

You can set small groups of picture thinkers to work with patterns for all the other numerals, or you can work together with each one as a class. Leave the results posted. Having all those patterns where they can be easily seen is important for picture thinkers. Leave them up for easy reference while you spend time with mental math stories. It's fine for students to glance at the patterns while working with mental math applications. You can give extra points for answers done with eyes shut if you want to, but, actually, the more children look at the patterns, the better.

Once the group reaches combinations that make 10, picture thinkers take readily to adding numbers like 18 + 22 by realizing that

18 is two 10's minus 2.
22 is two 10's plus 2. The 2's cancel each other.
That's the same as four 10's, or 40. How easy!

This seems roundabout, but anchoring number manipulations to the nearest multiple of 10 works well because it uses a set of relationships that can be seen in a flash. Picture thinkers get to be really quick with these "anchored relationships."

Emphasis on 10 is important because ours is a base-10 number system. Emphasizing 10 also leads naturally to a grasp of place value. Each place in the number system is a logarithmic progression: 1's, 10's, 100's, etc., another interesting pattern. If you want to introduce the Really Big Picture to some bright picture thinkers, you can add a decimal point and show how decimal numbers to the right follow the 10's pattern in ever tinier pieces, using the same tens' progression in the opposite direction. A glimpse is enough usually. You can come back to decimal operations another rung up the math ladder.

100's Charts

The 100's Chart is an essential piece of classroom equipment. It can be used in many, many ways. For example, it can be a number line. A large 100's chart posted on the wall can be a complex number line for counting, adding, and subtracting numbers from 1 to 100, moving forward or backward as needed anywhere horizontally along the chart. This supplants the large side-of-the-room walkable number line from 1 to 20 or so usually found in classrooms for young children. This same 100's chart can be used from kindergarten up all the way to factoring for fractions and algebra. Treasure it!

The 100's chart is big and complex enough for discovering a multitude of patterns. Using the overhead projector and a wipe-off 100's chart transparency, you and your class can have a lot of fun. Fun! That immediately engages picture thinkers.

Show a plain chart of numbers to begin with. Ask your class what patterns they notice. You will get all kinds of answers that will need to be discussed and validated. Some obvious ones are that in each column all numbers end with the number at the top of the column. Each number in each vertical column is 10 numbers apart. If you start at the upper left hand "1" and go diagonally downward, each number ends in order: 1,2,3, etc. This is also true if you move horizontally across each line. There are all sorts of things to discover. For instance, if you start at any number and move diagonally up to the left, you will be subtracting 11. If you move diagonally down to the right, you will be adding 11. Let them count this out to prove it.

You can also point out more complex patterns. For example, suppose your class collected 14 cans of food for a food drive. Someone brings in 7more cans. How many is that? You can start counting past number 14 to seven more places and you come to number 21. Further, if you had 24 cans to begin with and then counted 7 more, you would come to number 31. If you had 34 cans to begin with and counted 7 more, you would be at number 41. And so on. The pattern jumps right out at you. All kinds of patterns can be found and even color-coded. Taken together, these form an interwoven "big picture" for those picture thinkers. And the pattern is clear for sequential learners, too. Everyone benefits. You can runoff a gazillion hundreds charts that you keep handy for your students to play around with. Have highlighters, too. Students will discover all sorts of patterns that they can then share with others. Have a corner of the room where the discoveries are posted. You might have a place of honor for the pattern discovery of the day. Leave past discoveries posted. Have a variety of patterns derived from the 100's chart in plain sight. They are all interconnected because they come from the same basic chart. The more they are used, the more they form interwoven patterns in the visual memories of those picture thinkers (and some stepwise learners also). Now as picture thinkers begin to memorize specific facts, the patterns are in the background providing connections and the Big

Picture. Now, individual facts are more likely to stick. That's a plus.

The more they explore the charts and the more patterns they find, the more relationships are being entered into your students' mental computers. Pieces of the whole are being etched in memory and related to each other. After a while student—especially picture thinkers—will be able to refer to their visual memory rather than count on their fingers.

The fun goes on! Be sure to post all the patterns that various students discover in full view in all their color-coded glory. As the ideas of the hidden existence of patterns sinks in, picture thinkers develop an interior number lattice—a matrix of patterns that provides the needed framework to make memorization of math facts easier, if such memorization is attempted. The later in the process this happens, the better.

Different strokes for picture thinkers!

To review: For picture thinkers, attention needs to be drawn to all sorts of patterns and connections. They need to experience using the visible patterns in interesting and fun ways until the various combinations and their values are fixed in memory. This is the alternative way (to flash cards and drill sheets) of learning number facts for picture thinkers. Let me mention another idea here. A creative use of the calculator to aid memorization is to let it provide feedback. After adding or subtracting or whatever, immediately check the answer with a calculator. Pause a few nanoseconds and let satisfaction sink in. Yes, 15-8 is 7, just as you thought. If the answer is not correct, immediately see yourself mentally erasing the wrong answer and entering the right one: 15 – 8 equals 7. Enter that number sentence in your mental math storage area.

Gaming

So much for patterns, at least for now. What about games, another interesting and fun way for pictures thinkers to learn?

A game in hand is worth two or more worksheets in the bush or anywhere else. Picture thinkers, who love fun and games, really learn well under the competitive pressure of game playing. For those beginning stages where children are learning what number combinations equal "5" (or another numeral), games can provide practice. They put to use the knowledge just acquired, providing application, a higher-level thinking skill.

"Hit the Target" is such a game. It is very simple. A target number, like 5, is set. Each child draws 2 number tiles (dominoes or dice or a spinner can be used). Is there some way to add or subtract these numbers to equal 5? If so, we have a winner right away! However, this does not usually happen, and the game proceeds. Each child in turn draws 2 numbers and tries his or her luck. On the next round of turns, each child draws one more tile. Now there are more chances to make some of the numbers drawn equal 5. If someone has a winning combination, it can be checked out by the other players, using the 100's chart as a number line or using a calculator.

There are commercial games to buy, such as "Make 7," available from The Mindware Company (www.mindwareonline.com). But any number will do. It doesn't have to be "7." Set up a target number. Then have children and toss two or three dice or draw cards from a deck in turns. The goal is to be able to equal the target number by performing some kind of operation or series of operations that work with the numbers you have. For example, if "6" is the target, tossing the numbers "2," "3," and "1" would work by addition. Tossing or drawing "8" and "2" would work by subtraction. Any number can be the target. This game is even more fun to play as more and more operations are learned. It really fosters math reasoning and strategizing.

There are also traditional games to use. Cribbage is based on quickly being able to create combinations of 15. A game of cribbage, with 2 children playing and several kibitzing provides much better practice than worksheets that demand writing. For gamblers, there is Blackjack, where 21 is a number of importance, but you can create your own card game, where a group of children can try their luck at equaling any number you or they pick. Anyone who draws cards whose sum goes over the target number is out until the next game, but they are free to watch, help check answers, and learn.

In the beginning, "Hit the Target" can be used just for adding, with only lower number dominoes (or other number sources) put into the game. Later, the game can include larger numbers and both addition and subtraction. As each operation becomes familiar, multiplication, division, fractions, square root, etc. can be added. With more complex ways to "Hit the Target," a calculator can be the referee as to valid number combinations.

Place value in our base-10 system can be further clarified through the game of Chip Trading. Chip Trading uses a mat with three columns, one each for units, tens, and hundreds. Only nine chips can go in any one column – in our base 10 system. You can use this same mat for teaching other number systems. In a base 5 system, only four chips can be placed in the units column.

It also uses chips or tokens in three colors, one color for each column. The rule in base ten is that each column (or place) can hold up to 9 chips. If the number is larger than 9, 10 chips are subtracted and 1 chip (standing for that group of 10) is placed in the column to the left. So if your mat had 7 chips in the 1's column, and you drew an additional 5 chips by spinning a dial or casting a die, you would then be able to remove 10 chips, substitute 1 higher value chip that is placed in the 10's column, and have 2 chips remaining in the ones' column. That's why we write the number: 12 –meaning one 10 and 2 ones – in the way we do. Chip trading can be played in a group of 4 – 7 children, where each child has his or her own mat, a target number is set, say 25 or 40, and the children take turns tossing dice or spinning for a number and then growing the number on their mat. Children are engaged with each throw, checking to make sure each new addition is done right. Again, a calculator can be the judge.

Chip Trading can also be done with subtraction. Everyone starts with a number, like 25, and keeps subtracting according to the luck of the draw. The first person to reach zero or lower wins. Students can also watch the base-10 number system at work in their parents' cars by watching the mileage gauge, which proves the rule. They will see as they watch the numbers roll by that you cannot have a numeral higher than 9 in any column. That is the Base-10 Law!

In addition to card and board number games that provide sneaky drill, there are many software programs where number fact knowledge helps wins points. For picture thinkers, becoming good at these games accomplishes *automaticity* of math facts knowledge. It has the big advantage that it doesn't measure the ability to write numbers quickly but directly rewards knowledge of math facts. I do not think software games teach *how* to arrive at math facts well, but they do provide incentive to learn them and to get faster at their recall.

hundreds	tens	ones

2	4	9
hundreds	**tens**	**ones**
O O	O O O O	O O O O O O O O O

CHIP TRADING MAT

100's Charts and Multiplication

The 100's chart also helps when picture thinkers move into multiplication. Swift recall of multiplication facts is a sticking point for most picture thinkers. Because they see the relationships among things and understand systems, remembering isolated math facts is really hard, as was said earlier. Multiplication facts seem to be even harder to learn than addition or subtraction facts. They are less connected to acts of daily life, like making change. Picture thinkers can work hard at learning their times tables. They can take in the facts, but these don't stay glued in because they aren't connected to a larger system. They just sit there momentarily and then fly away.

Of course, you will want to begin with building the concept of multiplication with real objects, rows of real objects. You will want to use a variety of real objects and overhead items to show that multiplication is repeated adding. Base-Ten blocks are good for this, but so are M & m's or buttons. There are lots of commercial or teacher-made sets of counters to use. Graph paper can also be colored in and the squares counted. Children soon see the point and also see how cumbersome it is to do all that counting. They are ready to integrate those facts for quick recall, somehow. Still, even when motivated, step-by-step learners are naturally better at the memorization game than the visual-spatial picture thinkers, a fact of life that is discouraging for picture thinkers.

However, multiplication facts are fun to learn and are better learned by picture thinkers when they are learned as patterning. Here is where the 100's chart comes in, this time for skip counting. Provide each child with a stash of 100's charts and some variably colored highlighters. let them play around with setting up patterns. (Some will already have discovered skip counting as they searched for earlier patterns. That's fine. Just pull them out as samples.) Give each a child a handful of assorted highlighters and turn them loose, as you did earlier.

It's helpful to skip count each number in a different color of highlighter. Begin with one number and color. When skip counts of the second number in a new color land on the same numbers, ring the first number with the second color. If several numbers are done on the same chart, there will be some colored bull's eyes identifying popular numbers to land on. The whole pattern is getting to be complex, but is all the more interesting and memorable because of that. And the numbers with several colors will be helpful in teaching higher skills, like factoring.

You may want to have several large 100's charts on display: one with 2's, 3's, 4's and 5's skip-counted; one with 6's, 7's, 8's, and 9's. Or use any single display or combination of numbers that you choose.

The final flourish is to have a large 100s chart in the classroom where skip counting has been done (with the class periodically) with each number's skip counting in a different color. Begin with the 2's in pink, and then do 3's in violet, for instance. The trick here is to find see through highlighters in enough different colors. You might use water-color paints to make up the difference. (Keep this chart and pull it out again when you teach factoring!)

Your skip-counting display actually provides the basis for a multiplication facts chart now. It's time to convert from one to the other. Work with the class to fill out a large demonstration chart, either a large chalkboard grid or a grid on an overhead. Let the class help you fill in the numbers. They will be able to do the easy ones. They can also read the skip counts on the 100's chart to find the hard ones. When you are done, have your class indulge is a bit of constructionist (discovery) learning. Ask them to compare the products of 6 x

4 and 4 x 6; 8 x 7 with 7 x 8; 3 x 9 with 9 x 3, or whatever. You
don't have to go very far before they see the products are the
same whichever way you multiply. Let them check out other
combinations until they are sure. You can even tell them, "You
have just applied the commutative principle" which sounds
impressive.

All this lays the basis for Linda Silverman's strategy for
teaching multiplication facts to picture thinkers that she
included in *Upside Down Brilliance: The Visual-Spatial Learner.*
Linda begins by eliminating the 1's and 10's column because
they are super-easy. 1 times a number = that number. For 10 x
a number, you must add a zero. That done, you fold the chart
in half diagonally from the top left-hand corner to the bottom
right-hand corner. You do that because you have already
shown that the number set in one half equals its reverse in the
other half. 3 x 7 = 7 x 3 = 21. If you learn half the chart, you
already know the other half. That obviously makes the job
easier.

Linda goes on to explain that most children already
know how to count by 2's and by 10's. Counting by 5's is
another easy pattern to see, with 5's and 0's alternating in the
answers. This leaves a much smaller block of number facts
that will have to be committed to memory. Be sure to have fun
with the 9's pattern as a separate display:

The numbers in one column go up and the numbers in
the other column go down- NEATO!

$$2 \times 9 = 18 \qquad 6 \times 9 = 54$$
$$3 \times 9 = 27 \qquad 7 \times 9 = 63$$
$$4 \times 9 = 36 \qquad 8 \times 9 = 72$$
$$5 \times 9 = 45 \qquad 9 \times 9 = 81$$

The rule with multiplying 9's is to subtract 1 from the
number you multiply by (say you are multiplying by 6. 6-1 =

5. Then you see what number plus 5 equals 9. The answer is 4. So, 6 x 9 = 54. And so on. How cool! (Taken from Linda Silverman's guide to visual-spatial learners, *Upside-Down Brilliance*.)

There are several other tricks to apply, which you probably already know, such as the saying, "You have to be 16 to drive a 4 x 4." 4 times 4 = 16. The site at www.multiplication.com provides many memorization aides including silly stories. There are also tapes available where multiplication facts put to music may be just the ticket for some students. Others may like jump rope jingle versions of the facts.

Here is what Linda found to work, when getting down to the nitty-gritty work of actually memorizing those 8 to 15 stubborn facts not already learned. Her method involves using picture thinkers' strengths of emotional involvement in their learning and their love of pictures. The student tackles one fact at a time. Suppose that fact is 6 x 5 = 30. Linda has the child choose something he or she really loves, such as soccer, or chocolate cake or unicorns. Then she has the child draw a pattern that displays the fact — perhaps 6 pieces of 5-layer chocolate cake. Drawing all those layers in each of the six pieces of really yummy chocolate cake and writing that they all equal the number 30 really helps the fact stay in a picture-thinking mind. It is hugely superior to writing 6 x 5 = 30 over and over or doing many number drills where facts are jumbled together on a page. The child hangs the picture in a place where it will be seen for several days — perhaps the bathroom wall. Then it's on to the next troublesome fact. Remember, picture thinkers remember what they see (in relationship). They forget what they hear.

Memory for multiplication facts is also strengthened in the same ways that worked for addition and subtractions facts: games, patterns, and use in real-life situations. If a child is playing Math Blaster using multiplication facts, there is incentive to learn a pesky fact that keeps lowering the score.

Multiplication facts are also better learned by picture thinkers when they are coupled with division facts. This creates a more-complex, better remember set of relationships. The relationship fits a triangle. Commercial triangular flash cards can be purchased, or you can create a set easily. If you set your own triangle cards in this way, don't add operational signs. That way the triangle card can be used either for multiplication or division. For multiplication, the base of the triangle contains the two multipliers (or factors for later application). The apex contains the product. You can read the card either as "4 x 6 = 24" or "6 x 4 = 24." But you can also read it, starting from the top, as "24 / 6 = 4" or "24 /4 = 6." These seem to work better as memory refreshers after most of the multiplication facts have been mastered. They work better because they include a pattern relationship.

Math Vocabulary Words

This is something you are probably doing already for your math students. It involves setting up a wall chart with four parts — the four major operations of addition, subtraction, multiplication, division, and any other helpful terms. It probably includes such words as these:

ADD: and – another – put together – combine – add to – to – with – join- along with – too - also

SUBTRACT: less – more than – fewer – take away – lost – ended with – from – minus – leftover – less than – the rest – of - difference

MULTIPLY: times – rows – a minute (hour, day, year, etc.) – bunches – groups together

DIVIDE: each – how may groups – apiece – evenly – dealing out – between – into – among – divided up

EQUAL TO: as many – are – will be – is – the same –

They provide hints as to what operations to perform to solve the problem in what order and are helpful for all your students. Picture thinkers can add pictures to illustrate each operation or concept. They can draw or clip pictures that work for them that are kept in a folder where they work—their own handy reference! Or they can have their own stash of pictures for each operation, stowed away in envelope pockets.

Picturing Word Problems

Picture thinkers may grasp a concept immediately, especially when manipulatives or visuals accompany teaching. On the other hand, it may take then a while to get a math idea. When this happens, it does not help to repeat the first teaching. If it did not work in the first instance, a different approach is needed, not a repetition of what was said in the first place. Picture thinkers often need to see a thing from several angles. They need to have the new teaching connected to what they already know. When they haven't yet got the big picture, there is a need to ask a lot of questions and before that aha! insight comes. Once they get the idea, however, it is stored in their memories as a sharp image. It is important to know that, at that point, drill and practice do not improve the concept. In fact, the frustration of being drilled on the same thing over and over often leads to annoyance and anger (and errors).

Better than drill is the use of math word problems. These apply the new concept in a variety of ways, showing how it connects to everyday life and why it is worth knowing. Problems can be gleaned from math texts, teacher generated, or even put together by students themselves and shared with the class. They have the added advantage for picture thinkers of providing a bigger ratio of more thinking to less writing. While word problems are important for all students because they embed the math just learned into real life, promote thinking, and create math mastery, for picture thinkers they can be the difference between liking and hating math. However, because word problems are word problems, it is quite helpful for picture thinkers to be taught to draw or doodle pictures that represent the problem. That will help them set the problem up and solve it. We are back to seeing as a basic need for picture thinkers.

There is no "one way" to picture a word problem. Do encourage your picture thinkers to use whatever objects are at hand to "block out" the problem, like a stage director moving actors around. Or let them draw whatever helps them understand the problem. Even doodling is fine, if it works. There are commercial programs that help with picturing the problem and with learning to ignore unnecessary information. One such program is "Solving Word Problems with Pictures," available from PCI Educational Publishing. Drawing helps them — and you — see what they are thinking. They can also work in pairs and talk their ideas through with each other. They are trying to see the relationships in the problem, using their pictures and the math words in the Math Operations chare. That should help them see just what is being asked and how to reach an answer. They can also ask themselves if this problem is like any problem they have successfully solved in the past. What does it remind them of?

Sometimes it seems as if picture thinkers work best backwards. This is actually a good way for them to teach themselves something. They begin with the answer to a problem. They use the answer to see what process produced that answer, so that, another time, they will have a model to use if the same situation comes up. A similar strategy that works with all kinds of learners is to have a math kit that contains progressively harder story problems. Students work out the answers and then check an answer sheet to see if they are correct. This instant feedback lets them scrutinize their work to find their own error. Only if they are genuinely perplexed do they need a teacher's help. When they believe they have mastered a given level of problems, they can take a mastery test (teacher graded) to document their progress. Adding this component to your math program allows you as a teacher more time to help individual students.

Showing Your Steps

A perennial problem for picture thinkers is that math teachers so often insist that they show the steps of how they reached the answer to a problem, when they themselves are not conscious of any steps. They can only say, "I just know the answer, that's all!" Usually, a picture thinker truly does not know what steps were used to arrive at that answer. Picture thinkers are excellent at recognizing relationships and patterns, and mathematics is a set of special relationships that involve numbers. Picture thinkers often recognize the relationship and see the answer that goes with it. This is so obvious that it is really difficult to explain to someone else. We recommend that correct answers be given full credit.

Because some formal achievement tests now require problem solving steps to be shown, picture thinkers may require special teaching that helps them to deal with this special situation, while allowing them the freedom from this requirement otherwise. Alexandra Shires Golon, Director of Visual-Learners (www.visual-learners.com), has the following solution for picture thinkers, here paraphrased:

Go ahead and write down the answer that you know to be right. Work from that answer backwards to see how it might be possible to get from the end back to the beginning. Now you can write down the steps, this time going from the beginning to the end — the solution of the problem.

Of course, even better than this strategy is a situation where a teacher understands that a visual-spatial learner may not be aware of any steps taken and accepts right answers as the product of a real mental operation.

Some math textbooks, trying to encourage conceptual understanding of math rather than just memorization of methods, require written explanations of all the steps taken with a problem. This compounds the old "show your steps" problem, which before could be shown with numbers. Now sentences must be composed to create those mysterious steps — torture for picture thinkers. Yet focus on truly understanding the math you are using is a noble ideal. How can that be insured for picture thinkers?

Crystal Punch, a veteran math teacher, has used an excellent method to look at the reasoning that underlies problem solving and the variety of ways in which a problem may be solved. From the beginning, she involves her students — of all ages — in group discussion of possible math thinking. It is hard to underestimate the value of such sharing. This greatly aids estimation as well as promoting the concept that there can be multiple ways to solve problems. Crystal would start the ball rolling by setting up a problem. She might bring in a big jar of pennies and challenge, "How would you find out how many pennies we have here?" Hands go up and numbers are called out, which she writes on the board without comment: "62." "1000." "6 zillion." "Maybe 372." "I think it's 500 or 600." Every suggestion goes on the board. Then she will ask, "Rhonda, how did you decide on 1000? What was your thinking?" Rhonda's answer may be anything from a really wild guess, like the 6 zillion offering, or it may have a method: "I'm thinking about those rolls of pennies you get at the bank. I guess about twenty would fit in the bottom of the jar, standing on end. Then, you could pile maybe five sets on top. That makes 1000." Someone else may offer, "But these pennies aren't in stacks. They're all jumbled in together." Crystal asks, "Well, how did you come up with 500, Will?" The discussion is off, with students sharing their thinking with each other, beginning to discover that there are lots of things to think about in problem solving — so much more than just calculation.

Once such discussion has been introduced, it can become a routine, natural way to work. Students begin to think about what really does make sense. As they hear their classmates explain what each is thinking, they take in a variety of ideas, and are usually much more engaged than if the teacher is doing the explaining. Strategies will stick in these young minds to be tried later on. During such shared thinking times it helps to allow the calculators to come out, because the emphasis is on what might work, trying out new ideas, and maneuvering rather than exact calculation. It helps youngster think through whether it makes sense to have a multiplication word problem be a smaller answer than the number started with. Even children who don't volunteer answers are taking in many ideas about strategies and options. Number facts are tossed out and often better remembered for being used.

Such discussion is a basic teaching means that can continue on up from the elementary years through high school and beyond. Teachers can be quite aware of the quality of thinking of their students without having papers to grade. Math discussions are the basis of developing clear thinking about how to solve a variety of math problems. They stand out as a truly valuable teaching strategy.

Another method is to have students keep math journals, in which they demonstrate their understanding of whatever they are learning. Such journals may be either written words or numbers or a combination of both. This strategy allows each student to work from strength and also allows a teacher a quick peek into how much a child has followed the instruction given.

Fractious Fractions and Their Equivalents

There are a variety of fraction manipulatives available to help picture thinkers see the difference between whole numbers and their possible parts. Teacher or student-made fraction hands-on materials also work well. Children are used to breaking cookies in half or divvying up a pizza among friends, so fractions are easily recognizable as a possibility. Manipulatives make it clear that two fourths are exactly the same as one half because they overlay each other exactly.

Problems may arise, however, because we usually use the same size numerals to designate three classes of numbers when working with fractions. There are whole numbers, fraction numerators, and fraction denominators. At least to begin with, it is helpful to establish an arbitrary rule that whole numbers will be twice the size of the other numbers, while the fraction numerators and denominators will be half size and color-coded — say blue for numerators and red for denominators. Colored pencils or erasable colored pens can be used to carry out this theme.

That way, red will always stand for the number of divisions of one thing: fourths, halves, eights, etc., while blue will always stand for the number of those little pieces we are counting. This consistent plan makes the concepts involved in fractions very visible and easy to grasp. Again, we are looking at ways for picture thinkers to *see* the ideas they are presented with. It will, however, take a while for this or any system to become fully integrated and habitual. Human nature being what it is, it is probably better to teach the various fraction operations using easier-to-handle fractions, such as halves, fourths, thirds, rather than 32nds,164ths , and the like. When the emphasis is on the ideas of math, smaller numbers make the point better.

Reducing fractions has its own frustrations. It can be hard to see whether a given answer has been reduced to its simplest form. Of course all even numbers can be divided by two, which is helpful to remember and was visibly shown on that old 100's chart. It can take much time and confusion to try to see what other divisors might work. Finding the lowest common denominator (LCD) when combining fractions with unlike denominators is also tricky. It's the color-coded 100's chart to the rescue again. It can show what the possible factors are by looking at the common sites for various skip countings It is good to leave the chart up on the wall while working with LCDs.

Calculators are also helpful in this process. Using a calculator enables the problem solver to keep his or her mind on the aspect of the problem being worked on, while the calculator provides needed data. Later, when the concept is fully established, accurate calculation can become the focus.

There are also commercial excellent manipulatives to show equivalencies among fractions, decimals, and percentages. It's good to handle all three of these math areas as one: ways to work with parts of whole numbers. Our money system is helpful here. 100 pennies equal one dollar. Each penny is a hundredth of a dollar. That can be written .01 or 1/100 or 1%. A quarter equals 1/4 of a dollar (one quarter and one fourth mean the same thing). That can be written .25 or 25/100s or 25%. They all mean exactly the same thing but there are three systems to use. It's easy to see a game arising here, similar to "Go Fish." Index cards can be stamped with numbers in percent, fraction or percent form. The dealer begins, asking Player B, "Do you have any 50%'s?" If player B has that or an equivalent, he gets to take the dealer's card but must then ask another player for a specific equivalency. A reference chart with all equivalencies spelled out, can act as check point. Every time the chart is consulted, more memorization occurs.

Samples of steps/rules for multiplication or division of fractions need to be vertically visible. Picture thinkers need to see them to better remember and understand. Everyone will need lots of concrete examples of what dividing fractions means practically. "If you have pizzas enough for everyone to get ¼ of a pie, but then company comes so that there are twice as many hungry people, you will need to divide that portion, won't you? What would you do?"

Decimals can be taught as a special kind of fraction. They fit our base-ten number system. A highly visible wall chart with the names of the place numbers listed should be on the wall when working with fractions—helpful for everyone but essential for picture thinkers. That way it is easy to compare tens and tenths, hundreds and hundreths. The rules/algorithms for multiplying or dividing using decimals need to be easily seen, up on the wall.

Negative numbers

Picture thinkers easily understand negative numbers. They can *see* them all lined up below zero on the number line. They also grasp graphing and quadrants. Haven't they been playing killer Battleship for years? If not, they certainly should be. Most of the basics of geometry will be obvious to them, although there may be an initial struggle with the need to spell out the steps of their solution. This, again, may be a situation where they start with the solution they see and work their way backward to the beginning, in order to be able to state the steps.

www.khanacademy.org **is a wonderful online resource for visual thinkers featuring easy to follow instructions on every topic from simple addition to calculus.**

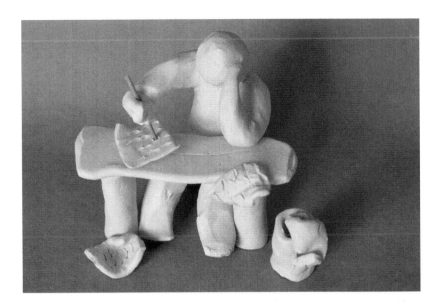

Chapter 6
Picture Yourself Teaching Writing to Picture Thinkers

Picture thinkers are full of wonderful stories. Their playful imagination and creativity make them natural story thinkers. Picture thinkers love nothing better than a good story. Give them a chance and they will tell it to you at length. Most are great conversationalists. Their verbal skills and strong vocabulary indicate their great narrative potential. Why then is it so difficult to get the story out of their imagination and onto the paper?

These natural story tellers have three bumps in the road to writing. First, their minds move too fast, with images racing through at breakneck speed. Second, they are not aware of sequence and organization but tend to put down whatever idea is passing through. They tend to write telegraphically, in short words and brief sentences, expecting the reader to imagine what is in the gaps. Third, the physical act of handwriting bogs down the process with coordination difficulties we are just beginning to be aware of.

These bumps are part of the spatial territory, native-born. Then, there is another problem that lies outside their control. That is the way we often teach writing.

Writing does not come naturally for picture thinkers if we instruct them in a step-by-step process. As you may have noticed, picture thinkers do not follow other people's stepwise thinking well. They are used to figuring things out for themselves. While they are born learners and deep thinkers, their ideas don't run in a straight line but blossom in all directions in technicolor and with emotion. They are empowered differently.

Teaching them as though they are sequential thinkers is not a win-win situation. If we do so, we ask them to relate to writing as though they could dissect their visions and feelings into separate pieces where there was once a complete, holistic picture. This wrong turn systematically shuts them down by draining their enthusiasm. Instead of teaching spatial learners by analytic, sequential methods, we need to turn them on to exploring their own ideas and fully capturing the life of their own minds. They need to write in their own way.
These are our kids who may not color inside the lines. Yet, while it is hard to get them to write an outline, use punctuation, or spell correctly, they may already have completed a small novel in their imagination. It is time to embrace learning differences and use techniques that bring out the very best of these bright minds.

Remember what their strengths are? Vivid imagery, enthusiasm, thinking outside the box, memory for experience, playfulness, and an imagination that doesn't quit.

The writing process begins at a different place for these creative children. It begins with what they do best, shows them what great writing potential they have, and uses techniques that provide help for their weak areas. This approach is also fun for more sequential students, who enrich their own writing experience through this innovative approach.

These ideas are not entirely new. Many of you may be using them now. They just have been considered more like a creative side-trip than "real" writing. For spatial writers, they are the royal road to success and well worth using.

Let's get more specific about what works.

There are many creative teachers who entice kids to write by exploring their feelings and senses. Writing is not a chore but an adventure. Spatial kids rejoice in these classes and begin right away to see themselves as successful writers. This whole approach might be called writing from the heart. It frees the child up to write to share the experience of the moment (even if called up in memory) in fresh and lively words—the words that are felt and lived just them. And, remember, writing from the heart works for both left and right-brain kids.

In these classrooms, there is an atmosphere of encouragement and feedback. Spelling, grammar, and punctuation take a back seat to vision, wisdom, and original thoughts. The environment is one where it is safe to ask questions, or even get stuck (which is often part of the process). New ideas, exciting words, and lively writing are praised, read aloud, and given places of honor on the walls for all to see. The writing is shared with authentic audiences. It is cherished and valued. Such writing has a purpose, which is to be heard and read by an audience.

Writing From the Heart

Writing from the heart, writing what they feel and find important, is the key to turning reluctant spatial learners on to writing. Once they know they can stir others with their words on the printed page, they are open to developing this talent.

Ideas that work for spatial writers are simple, and you may have already incorporated many of them into your classrooms. However, as Crystal has watched kids and adults struggle to write, she has come to know that we are not doing enough at any level to support this innate, important human need, and Betty agrees. To write is to communicate our thoughts, feelings, and visions for all to know. Every human being has the need to be understood, and while writing is not the only vehicle for communication, it is a vital one.

The first clue for success in writing is that, for visual-spatial learners, it is best to begin with short, intensely felt writing. It simply works better for those whose emotions are intertwined with all they do. First, brief writing focuses attention. If you are remembering and writing about some experience you felt with your whole body, you will be in that moment, reliving what you felt then. If that moment stopped you in your tracks, you will find that words are immediately there. While helpful for most writers, for picture thinkers this kind of remembered intense emotion is essential to opening the writing door. Keep the writing short and encourage genuine emotion, while also allowing the free flow of fun and experimentation.

Second, because writing is kept short, authors are not writing a lot of words. Yet their writing is effective and often admired by others. Brief, intense writing works well even when writing is difficult and awkward. Writers are in the moment, just getting the words down to capture them while they are hot. They know they can rearrange and refine them later, if necessary.

Third, writers quickly come up with a product that is full of life, captures feelings, and is engaging to read. They are instant authors! Furthermore, there is always the possibility they can add decorations, illustrations, color, and design to their exciting productions.

Using the strengths of picture thinkers just makes sense when we consider the bumps in the road they have to overcome. Start them writing from their emotions, and they will have fun and a great product. Have them write about what is funny, silly, magical, wonderful, sad, a once-in-a-lifetime experience, something they are passionate about. Keep the writing short and descriptive, the shorter the better. The single most important thing we can do as teachers is to give our students successful writing experience that builds the confidence they need to love writing.

So we will begin—shortly—with many ideas for brief, intense bursts of writing that are full of life and highly readable. But even before we do that, it is helpful to build writing vocabularies by paying attention to the wonderful world of words. This has probably been a classroom experience from day one. Vocabulary building is an essential part of teaching and learning. As your students remember vibrant experiences, you want them to have words at hand to use that can help others feel what they felt.

Here are some ideas to help with that vocabulary building. You undoubtedly, also have your own favorites.

Living Words

Vocabulary building goes on in a classroom much of the time, from the early grades onward. Often teachers will have a display of new, interesting words posted in a way to catch students' attention. This may be a "Wall of Words," bubbly "Word Balloons," cliché substitutes labeled "Say It Another Way," or a special word that is "Prize Word of the Day." Everyone tries to use that prize word in conversation that day. Students are encouraged to bring new words to the class's attention, and there is ongoing praise for using new words in either conversation or
writing.

There is great satisfaction and accomplishment in finding just the right words to describe what you are seeing, thinking or feeling. It's the same satisfaction an artist feels who finds just the right shade of color, the right angle, or good amount of light for a painting.

Still Life with Senses

Another way to focus on sensory words is to describe a still life or object that is set up for the class to view. A still life is motionless, so it is possible for writers to take their time and include all the details involved. The teacher models this process first, describing the scene in detail and listing each of the senses on her fingers. The teacher can also scribe sentences that describe the still life, taking everyone's suggestions and writing them on an overhead or on large paper for everyone to see.

For further practice, other still lifes can be constructed, using objects already in the room. This is a great activity for small groups as well as the entire class. Such activities are ongoing, because vocabulary building never stops. Whatever device you use to call attention to words, the heart of a successful program lies in the attention and notice given to words. There is no royal road to word wizardry, only continual paying of attention to word choice and its effectiveness

Sensory Stations
Setting up sensory stations in the classroom has been done for quite awhile. We are going to add words that fit each sensory station as they are discovered and post them on the wall for all to see and use.

Five finger senses: We have five wonderful senses that help us take in what we see or feel. Words that explain our senses can be quite fun to find, hear, and write. The fingers on a hand can be used as a great reminder to include all the senses when we write about something. Ask your students to review their senses on their fingers when they write. Have they used all the senses possible?

We talk to students about engaging their senses, but getting the feeling of those senses captured in words requires practice. Sensory stations are fun, provide immediate experience, and link to discovering and even creating words that help others share that experience. Young writers can draw upon this when writing and thinking about details and juicy words. Sensory stations help them discover what can make their descriptions "full of life."

Touch Center
Include various liquids such as warm water, soap, cooking oil, cold gelatin (and paper towels for sticky fingers).

The students love the variety of temperature and thickness of the liquids. Textures: rough, smooth, furry. The words and pictures they use to describe the experience are jewels. Use the sticky notes to create a word bank of fun adjectives. Post them in a cluster at the station.

Sound Center

Provide a variety of percussion instruments and recordings of music—or ordinary sounds—birds chirping, dogs barking, talking, whistling, thunder, rain, a motor running, brakes squealing, etc. Have a tape recorder to record the descriptive words they come up with. Or you can scribe directly onto those sticky notes.

Taste Center

Let your imagination go wild- sweet, sour, spices, foods and drinks that blend flavors, bad flavored jelly beans. Avoid things that might cause allergies, such as peanuts. Have toothpicks for dipping and tasting things.

Smell Center

Leftover school lunches, flowers, lemons, wet fur, bubble gum, spices, aromatherapy oils— there are so many possibilities. Have cameras ready for students to take pictures of using their senses. Post with the words that go with the pictures. Also have a collage of sticky –note words.
Idea: It is possible to combine the Taste and Smell Centers, so that things are smelled and then tasted. These two senses are very intertwined.

Sight Center

Bring in pictures to describe—photos. Ask your students to bring in a couple of family pictures or memories. Pictures taken from magazines work well also. Have a variety of objects to describe, apples, erasers, metal, flowers, dirt, murky water, glass crystals, microscopes might be fun to get a closer look at some of the items. Include color swatches, print designs, fluorescent items. Garner those stickies with their words and display them.

The idea is to keep changing and adding to the posts until you have your walls filled with fun, exciting, descriptive words that can be used when your students are writing. When you have finished going through the sensory stations, the class should have a huge selection of words for each sense, as well as a wealth of words from other vocabulary projects.

Here are a few more ideas to stimulate the writing process:

Word bubble up

The idea is to let your mind drift to words that describe the subject and create images. You are going into a creative mode that accesses your feelings and words that go with the situation. You can actually draw bubbles around clusters of words that seem to go together. This helps prime the pump for writing and aids the creative process.

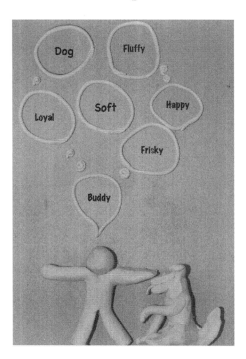

Jumping to a memory

Look at any object in the room. Then let that remind you of something else and let that something else leapfrog to another memory until something pops up that you want to write about. For example, you might look at the pencil sharpener. That might remind you of the tree that a pencil came from, which might remind you of walking in the woods, which might then remind you of a time when a squirrel came right up to you and wasn't afraid at all — a magical moment to write about.

Doodling or drawing to see if a story idea comes through

Sometimes just moving a pencil around on paper can start up the story telling process. There is a process of deliberately making many loopy scribbles on a piece of paper and then filling in some of the shapes that emerge to create an actual picture. This, in turn, may open to a story.

Cartoon Conversations

Cartoon characters can be cut out and silly conversations set up in the usual cartoon "balloons." Encourage your students to write funny conversations between all sorts of things, such as a pair of socks, a pencil and some paper, toothpaste and teeth, etc. They can either draw the objects and use cartoon balloons, or they can write this as a play script with a speaker's column and the exact words said set off in a wider column on the paper. No quotation marks are used, of course, for either cartoons or play scripts. It is easy for students to see the exact words said. When they come to write conversation in stories, they can learn to put quotation marks around the words that would go in a balloon if a cartoon character said them (or an actor in a play).

Some other ideas for brief writings are: commercials, guess what I am thinking, descriptions. If your students get stuck trying to begin their writing, they might try the "word bubble up" plan or talk aloud with a writing partner to generate ideas.

Writing large to small

Now that the students have a sense of descriptive language and juicy word choices, we can turn to another writer's challenge: sentence order in a paragraph. We are introducing the idea of a main or topical sentence for a paragraph. Descriptions that work from large statements to smaller details are important in organizing a paragraph. Try taking a few detail sentences and saying them in random order. Can students guess what you are talking about? Why or why not? Describing from a large idea to smaller details is one important step toward organizing a paragraph.

Students often write about a subject beginning with the details. For example, writing about a picnic, they might mention such ideas as "...there were lots of ants and we had potato salad the wind blew the napkins all over the park..."Sometimes it is helpful to ask them to think of a title. You can also teach them to write "Big to Little." This means writing a lead sentence, which can be the start of the paragraph. That would involve taping the lead sentence at the start of the paragraph. Eventually, your writers will get the idea that they need to begin a paragraph with the "big" (general) ideas and then fill in the details.

With your class, practice creating a main idea for a given picture or idea students have been working with. The idea is to "Think Big First!" Ongoing practice will be needed by the whole class to build in this attitude. There are several ways of providing practice. Here are a few:

- Worksheets with main sentences in one column and detail-only paragraphs in another column. The students are to find matches. Discuss: how hard is this to do?

- Telegraphing information. Words cost money here. The most important information is what needs to be sent.

- Writing captions for pictures. There is a limited amount of space for a caption.

- Sorting out a photo album. This, again is attaching needed information to pictures.

Here is another idea to aid the effectiveness of descriptions. Your students can take turns describing an object to their classmates who cannot see what is being described. See if the class can draw what is described from what they are hearing. This is similar to tasks where students describe a "How to do something, step by step" and see if the class can follow along. An underlying goal should be for students to see that beginning with a main idea helps others understand the rest of the paragraph.

Word play with senses and feelings

These activities overlap with vocabulary building. They continue the focus on word power and open into playful, experimental, and interesting writing products.

Word Collages

There are no set rules here, only a slew of creativity and experimentation. One way to begin is to make little word arrangements. Have students copy words they love from stickies in the Sensory Stations section of the room. Challenge them to arrange a layout of the words to create a feeling or mood. They can add drawing, stamps, designs, color, cartoons, etc. to make the collage come alive. Such an activity teaches directly the power of single words to evoke feelings. A gallery of such collages is a wonderful display of creativity.

Word Bubbles

Similar to collages, but words are arranged in bubbles,

like the ones cartoon characters use when speaking. You can have a "bubble" conversation. Students can draw or cut out two characters that might be having this talk and attach the bubbles.

One Moment in Time

Tell about when: you lost a tooth, you slipped in the mud, you thought you were lost, a horse ate out of your hand, you found a new friend...

Poetry Forms

Like beginning each line with a letter from your name, a formula like "I used to be ____ but now I'm ____," diamontes, haiku, anything you or students design.

Word Mobiles

Arranged thematic words hanging from a hanger. Can you title this?

Walking Down Memory Lane

Brief sentences beginning, "Walking down Memory Lane, I saw rainbows in the drops shaking from the trees," "Walking down Memory Lane, I smelled the road tar melting in the hot sun," etc.

Some other ideas are:

Lyrics for tunes, pearly words on a string, memory lane phrases as captions for pictures, word slams, and concrete poetry (simple drawings in which words are embedded in a drawing, like a snail with words in a coil, a cat with a cat-words outline, a plant made up of descriptive words)... More advanced brief writings could be a scene from a dream, a vivid brief memory, a mood evoker...You have your own favorite writing stimulants. Just use them!

The Magic of Freeze Frame

Such word writing experiments lead to other writing challenges. For wildly imaginative spatial learners, a major challenge is capturing their fleeting ideas and images with their often quite slow handwriting. We offer a new and wonderful technique to deal with this problem. Its name is **Freeze Frame**, and it is the key to manageable writing for picture thinkers.

Picture thinkers come in many varieties, but they all think in images, feelings, and videos that move very quickly. Often the usual bloom of ideas spreads out in all directions at the same time. How can anyone write that down? Even when picture thinkers can *see* what they want to say, they still need to convert everything into words while their mental movies are racing ahead. What a challenge! This inability to keep up with their speed of thought is possibly the most frustrating thing about writing for picture thinkers.

These images, ideas, and feelings of a picture thinker flit, flutter, and speed through consciousness at an incredible rate. Freeze frame can be a great help here. Rather than worrying about forgetting ideas or parts of the story, writers can relax and feel confident that their ideas are held to come back to. It gives them time to follow whatever technique they are developing for writing. No longer do they lose their place as fifty other things sweep through their minds.

Realize what is going on. Picture thinkers literally have to slow down and stop their images to describe them. They need to search for the right words to use, while in the meantime, the mental movie has changed from scene to scene, changing the story line. They have to pull their mind back 15 or so thoughts to where they were when they started writing; a sequential task that really is difficult for them. Then the thought disappears while that search goes on.

This is really a technical problem. The writer needs a way to slow down or stop the rush of images. Our familiarity with movies, videos, and TV's provides us with a simple solution to the "image that got away" problem. The Pause button works with electronic equipment. We can also press "Pause!" when writing. That means bringing in freeze frame to the rescue. Freeze frame stops time and helps expand the moment to make it long enough to write down the details that make for rich writing.

Let's see how to use freeze frame. Writers can pick a particular subject to write about and draw a quick sketch or symbol that stands for that moment. The drawing goes in front of their writing screen or at the top of the paper, so when they write their ideas are held in place by the picture. The picture is the freeze frame. One freeze frame might represent a paragraph, with its main idea. Several freeze frames can stand for the ongoing events or story line. You focus on one sticky at a time when you write.

Wow! We can stop time!

Here are some ways of introducing this idea:

Play classroom Freeze Tag. At intervals during regular activities, sound a note. Everyone freezes in place. Show a movie and stop the film, freezing it.

Have students volunteer to produce a short skit and "freeze" at intervals.

Ask your students to bring in photographs of themselves doing something at a particular event, the more stop-action the better. Or take pictures of students in action in the classroom. Start a picture section of "expressive moments."

Each time, make the point, "We can stop our action. We can freeze time. It gives us a chance to stop and see all the details of what's happening, and what could happen next. We can also do this when we write. It puts the writer in the Director's Chair, to create and plan. You can enrich these moments by having students look around them and focus on someone or some action. What do they think that person is thinking right now? How are they feeling? What are they going to do next? What if they did something else? Then what would happen? Discuss what that experience was like for the class. What did they discover?

Now begin to use freeze frame and its magic with writing. It is good to continue with brief, emotional writing, perhaps doing "One Moment in Time," as a class project. Provide each child with a sticky note and writing paper. Take a minute while each remembers something that jumps into their mind. Then follow these steps:

Make a quick sketch — stick figures, symbols, whatever — to stand for that experience on the sticky. Put it at the top of the writing paper.
Go back into your remembered moment. Let all your senses feel deeply what you experienced before. Soak up the atmosphere. See and feel again what happened.

Now, write down everything you saw and felt in your moment. Take your time. If your mind races ahead, just look at your sticky note. It holds down the main idea for you. You can take as long as you need to put in all the feelings and details. Use the best words you can think of. You are the Director, making your moment come alive for others to experience also.

Rome wasn't built in a day, and practice will be needed to develop fully the power of writing in extended time, focused by freeze frame. Reading aloud and sharing the really good writing that can happen through this technique helps students realize its potential. Be sure to exhibit these writings and honor them.

Here is an example of talking your class through writing up a moment:

The photo on display is of a student whose nose is wrinkled up smelling an old lunch bag (from the Smell Center). What are some ideas? Talk and elicit the children's ideas also: That student is full of life because he is smelling the old lunch, he thinks it is icky, the bag feels used and crinkly in their hand, he sees the contents, and they are gross! You can write these down on chalkboard or overhead, inserting new words, crossing out if wanted. Messy is all right at this stage. The picture helps them hold their focus, even if the discussion takes several minutes.

Encourage students to be in the Director's Chair and rearrange their sentences if they see a better way to create the memory. Model this in your own examples. They do not have to write to do this. Let them use scissors and glue sticks to rearrange. (This echoes what a word processor—a huge boon for spatial learners—can do with editing.) Once the arrangement is just right, with words spelled correctly, the final product can be copied and illustrated.

Another problem for picture thinkers is capturing everything they see and hear and feel on paper. They tend to omit writing down many of the details that are in the picture in their mind's eye. One reason for this is that picture thinkers assume that you see exactly what they see—all the sensory details—even though they aren't actually writing them down. Because of this, their writing lacks exactly those details that would give it life. When they read what they have written, they see the same sensory details that were in their mind when they wrote. That makes it hard for them to understand you are talking about when you say details are missing. You may have to ask them, "Where does it actually say that in your writing?"

Yes, picture thinkers often miss the most obvious parts of descriptions. Stopping time with freeze frame allows them the time needed to focus and write. The snapshot of time can be examined and fully described. The writer can look closely at the idea or scene, see the big picture and then fill in the details, layering in the senses, and emotions. Like looking back through photo albums, the pictures can be enjoyed and added to at a leisurely pace, because the freeze frame also serves as a book mark or "thought mark" for the story.

Freeze frame can enable the movement from very brief, heartfelt writing to more elaborate memory writing. Once the trick of holding focus is established, you can move on to the second major writing road bump, the problem of organization.

Beginning, Middle, and End: Organizing Writing

Now your class is moving from brief writing to writing stories with a beginning, middle, and end. The idea of focused freeze frame writing can be extended to work here also. This poses two areas of difficulty. One is organizing thoughts sequentially, a trail of sticky notes with their idea pictures can provide a plan to hold to.

When planning a story to write, have your students draw pictures on sticky notes that stand for the main parts of the story. Then they should create an arrangement of the freeze frames stickies that makes sense to them. This will:

- Provide an overview of the story line
- Hold their focus on each idea as they write
- Give them time to organize their thoughts and add the needed rich detail as they write
- Act as a place holder to come back to – hold thoughts in place

If your students have created word banks for a variety of senses and emotions, your writers can use these to create specific word lists to help them describe their story. This can help if they are stuck at the very beginning of their writing. Sometimes percolating words lists to capture the essence of the story unlocks the story flow. The words chosen help convey the background ambiance and lead the writer to begin writing.

Freeze frame ideas to get started

Illustrating the idea of a single frame or single slice of time can be fun and engaging for all students.

- Show them a movie and stop the film- essentially "freezing it"
- Stop in the exciting part of a book and have your students freeze the moment and then describe it.
- Have students create a short skit and have them freeze at points throughout the skit.
- Set a buzzer to go off at random times in the classroom and have students freeze the moment.
- Take pictures of the moment and check the accuracy of the recall of details
- Have a "thief" run through the class dressed in unusual clothing and disguise to see if your students can remember the event and its details.

For any of the above events, hand everyone a sticky note or slip of paper and have them draw quick ideas about the moment. They will need enough ideas to re-create the moment in words later. Students love to share their sticky notes and describe what they "captured" on paper.

One way to begin is to have your students briefly sketch a scene they have visualized. We are not trying to capture artistry as much as we are gathering details, the sketch can look like a kaleidoscope of ideas and feelings about the moment. Whatever works works.

Introducing a Single Frame or Slice of Time

Freeze frame holds the focus by using a small picture — a thumbnail sketch on a sticky note — to keep ideas from running away. This seemingly simple device is a huge help for picture thinkers. Its use opens the door to many kinds of writing later on.

I often describe freeze frame as if my mind is taking a photograph like a camera and I am looking at the *all* of the detail, recalling the events, emotions, and the whole moment.

Take several photos of yourself and the students in your classroom. Describe the events that were taking place as you see them in the photo and as you remember them happening. I go into much detail about a photo being two dimensional and the activity being full of life. Asking the class this question "What does full of life mean? " gets your students to construct a description that uses all of their senses and range of emotions. As you begin to detail what "full of life "means in each photo, you begin to look at how each sense is used, as well as the motion and emotion of the story.

Ask your students to bring in photographs of themselves at a particular event or doing something. Bring in some photos that you have at home or better yet, take photos of the students in your classroom engaged in various activities and conversations. Look through magazines for pictures. Start a classroom collection of expressive moments. These can be used as stimuli for producing many juicy descriptive words.

Next, work with your class using any familiar story, such as "Stella Luna   " Have your students describe something that they hear in this story (or you can start with any of the senses). Then go to the story itself. Ask the students for sentences that tell the story. Write these(preferably on an overhead transparency). Are these sentences in the right order? Cut them up and move them around on an overhead until there is agreement on the order. This is the framework of the paragraph. It is possible to draw a sketch that will stand for the idea of the "Stella Luna" Now we can go back and add details or juicy words to the picture.

The idea of drawing a sketch on a sticky note that can represent an idea or a story is an important one. This sketch is a frame that holds the story or a part of the story in place. Frames can be manipulated into various arrangement. A single frame can be used to focus the attention (stop time) while writing, which is extremely helpful. You are building this concept with your class, whether you work with "Stella Luna" or some other well-known tale.

Once you have described this process of creating a frame to your whole class, they can work in small groups and make their own freeze frames, getting feedback from their peers about whether they have included enough details in their sketches.

Now that they have had practice creating a freeze frame, students can next make several freeze frames and move them around to form a story order. This is a basic and important step toward organizing their writing, which is otherwise so difficult for picture thinkers. When they do the thinking pictorially, the process makes more sense to them.

The idea is that anyone can write in a focused manner about a sticky note, often one paragraph to a note. Then the paragraphs can be put together to form a story or article. Of course, it is necessary to add bridging words or phrases so that the whole piece of writing makes sense.

Although this process of writing to sticky notes often creates a mess: crossed out words, taped sentences, added or bridging words scribbled in the margins. However, the author (and others) should be able to read the story even though it does not look good. And the story is ready to be copied neatly — typed if possible — with confidence. If a word processing program is available, editing becomes easy and the mess is eliminated.

Having the story read aloud would be motivating to the students. This can lead to a student typing the paper, or it can be scribed be scribed by someone. This could even lead to the motivation of turning the whole thing into a book — recopying it perfectly with illustrations that go along with the story. Oral presentations, coffee house readings etc. are all fun ways to honor the authors in your room.

Freeze Frame: " Using the Time Stopper"

Stopping time — why do we want to stop time? The idea is to hold the focus while you write. Otherwise thinking moves too rapidly. Ten ideas flit by before you have written the first two words. This problem becomes even more acute if writing is awkward and slow for you.

Help is needed. The details that make writing come alive need time to be examined to capture them, to include all the magic of the senses. Or, if you are using visualization to stimulate your ideas — which is a very good thing to do — that will also take time. A way is needed to hold focus even though the mind may be flying off in all directions- so you can take in everything that is there or be a fly on the wall. Freeze Frame is the answer to this problem. It holds your focus as you write. Not only does Freeze Frame aid intense focus, it works to overcome distractibility. If your mind slips away, that is okay. Freeze Frame will bring your mind right back and allow you to take the needed time to collect all of the details that make writing come alive.

Additionally, freeze frames can be arranged into a series that can provide a quick outline for your story or paper. Freeze frame arrangements hold your thoughts in place as you write. Moreover, the arrangement is fluid; it can easily be revised. Another benefit is that a writer can pick a frame and begin writing from any part of the story, which is quite appealing to visual-spatial learners and other out-of-the-box thinkers. You do not need to be an artist to use freeze frame. The frames are usually just scribbled sketches or symbols of an idea.

Planning Boards
Time is what prevents everything from happening all at once – John Archibald Wheeler

As an educator, Crystal often took for granted that terms such as sequence (beginning   middle- end), order, organization, and time made sense to everyone, and that they operated using these ideas on a daily basis. It took a while to see the disconnect and understand that these "basic concepts" were not basic or part of the foundation of the imaginative picture thinkers she was teaching. There are two issues. The first is that details clearly visible in the children's minds were not clearly visible on paper to the reader. They hadn't written them down because all this seemed so natural to them (like the ocean to fish) that they assumed others saw what they saw in their imagination. Every time they re-read their writing, they mentally saw the same details vividly. They didn't realize these were actually missing in their writing.

The second issue is that, for picture thinkers, everything happens all at once. They see the end at the same time as the beginning when they think of an event. It's like a cake, where the beginning is mixed into the whole batter, like raisins. They have an emotional sequence they follow that is full of drama, humor, and suspense, but it is not necessarily time-related so that the story can nicely jump over it all. Since they think the storyline is the big events, the drama, the emotion, and the solution all stirred in together, how can they be helped to write so the story can be followed by the reader?

Crystal likes to share flipbooks with her students. They can watch the story unfold as the pages turn. It's easy to see that there is a beginning, middle, and end. They are physically part of the book itself. The flow of movement would be interrupted if we changed the order; the story would fall apart. Then she explains that the same thing is true for stories they write. The flipbooks make a strong point.

You can help the class see the defining spaces of beginning, middle, and end by reading or presenting short stories that flow from start to finish. Forget about flashbacks at this point! Like the flipbooks, the movement needs to be uninterrupted. After the story, discuss with them what part was the beginning, the end, the middle. A discussion where they hear other children's ideas about these divisions helps them realize this is a judgment call, but also helps them see that it is quite important that the beginning, middle, and end be there.

When you feel most children get the sequence of BME, it's time to put the skill to use in writing a very short story. You can have them retell a story they know, or create a new one. You can also use a memory of something that happened that they would like to write about. You want to keep this very short, one page or less, but at least three paragraphs long. Very importantly, you want to draw on spatial strengths as you develop the non-spatial skill of writing serially.

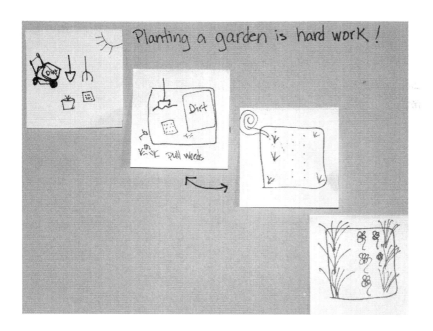

Because picture thinkers have already learned to do brief, "from-the-heart" writing with a single Freeze Frame picture, it's good to start there. You can use the power of Freeze Frame writing to help them create an excellent BME story. First, have your writers choose 3 to 5 important moments from their story and draw a Freeze Frame picture for each on a sticky note. Then have them will try different arrangements of these 3 to 5 stickies until they find an order that makes sense to them.

Before the actually writing begins, feedback can be quite helpful. Have writers share their planned arrangement with a friend. If a peer can understand the pictures and follow their arrangement, it is okay. If there is confusion, either better important moments need to be chosen, or the order needs to be revised. Peer review is a big step to reducing frustration once the actual writing begins. As with any artist, it is easier to talk about ideas and possibilities before production. Once the piece has been completed, when they have already put in a tremendous amount of effort, writers are likely to be quite sensitive to criticism.

When pictures and their order make sense to a peer, writers then make a quick sketch of each freeze frame picture in the right order on a planning paper. *This is actually a picture outline for the story.* The planning paper goes in the student's story folder.

Think what we're doing. Children arrange one freeze frame moment next to another until they have a whole story. No writing has happened yet (except for possible words that might go with some sticky pictures). Yet they have a whole story in front of their eyes. Beginning, middle, and end are all there.

Now it is time to begin writing. As children begin to write, the stickies will hold the plan together. This leaves the writer the magic of stopping time one picture at a time and adding all the wonderful details for each in that timeless "now" in which he or she so naturally works. Freeze frame to the rescue!

The writer can choose which picture to begin with. Because the order is fixed on the planning sheet, any picture can be written about first if the writer chooses to. The chosen sticky is peeled away from the writing plan and stuck to the top of a piece of writing paper. Or it can be quickly copied onto another sticky, which becomes the freeze frame focus for writing completely about that picture. Previous freeze frame practice now creates the technique of the writer being immersed in the picture—to see, feel, smell, hear, and experience—what is going on. There is plenty of time to include all the juicy details so others can read the words and see all that the picture stands for.

At the same time, the writer can use all the props you have posted to facilitate good writing: the collection of exciting, interesting words; visualization prompts, and the questions that remind you as a writer to include everything you see and experience in your freeze frame deep focus.

The overall technique is this: A single piece of paper is used for each freeze frame moment, which becomes a paragraph. When each moment has been transformed into words, with spelling and punctuation edited and complete, the paragraphs can be cut away from unused paper. Then the paragraphs are pasted together in the planned order on a new piece of paper to create a real story with a beginning, middle, and end. Any needed bridging words can be added. Freeze frame helps ensure that the writing is rich, detailed, and juicy. This is exactly the way a word processor works: you write, edit, cut, and paste. The process works for picture thinkers.

You can picture it all going on. During story writing time, each student has something to write about, and is familiar with a technique to help focus and include the details that make writing rich. Many will want to use words they don't know how to spell. As with the earlier, heartfelt writing practice, allow them to quietly come to you and ask for correct spelling; you simply print the word quickly on a sticky or other scrap of paper. If a long line forms, teach them to write the first and last letter they hear in the word and leave enough space to write in the whole word later. That way they can continue writing until you are able to give them the word. If you have an aid or a parent volunteer, this is a great job to delegate to them. There may even be super speller students who would like to provide spelling words. Your judgment is key as to whether you want to allow this or not.

You, as teacher, circulate, trying not to interrupt focus, but available if any writers have questions for you or want you to admire what they have done. You may even have time to jot down some super sentences that you want to share with the whole class as samples of good writing. You can see how positive an experience this group writing session can be.

Non-fiction writing for the picture thinker
Now, we go a step beyond. We have done brief, emotionally charged writing that helps picture thinkers discover their inner writer. They have actually written good stories that have a beginning, middle, and end. We are ready now, and only now, to tackle the considerable challenge of a written research report.

Non-fiction writing, for picture thinkers, is the first type of writing that is *outside their own experience.* What makes picture thinkers wonderful at telling stories is their ability to put themselves in the story as it takes place. But non-fiction writing usually deals with something that is unfamiliar. This makes writing difficult because picture thinkers cannot draw from their experience and, unlike when writing science fiction, they can't just make up some new reality out of their imagination. They know they are supposed to write about something real. They struggle with deciding what is important to say and even how to begin because they do not have personal experience with the subject and have no basis for judgment.

One answer is for them to begin writing about something they do know about. This might be a hobby or something they are really familiar with, such as taking care of a gerbil or handling a paper route. However, if you are trying to teach them how to write a report about new material that they have researched, there is this special problem that needs to be addressed: How do you help them actually experience what it would be like to be living inside their subject?

Write about what interests you

Giving your students the chance to pick their subject, whatever kind of non-fiction writing assignment it is — biography, learning about a state, or finding out about a process — will go better. It will enhance their motivation and buy-in. Anything they already know about their topic or any way they can relate to it gives them a foot in the door. Otherwise, you will need to help them gain some kind of experience or feel for the subject. Watching movies about the time period involved can provide them with memorable visuals and general ideas. If you are studying early settlers, try panning for gold, or invite an old timer as guest speaker. Consider connections to music, clothing, food, religion, etc., that can help build experience for the writer to connect with and draw on.

Encourage your picture thinkers to approach picking resources for writing assignments as fun. Have them visit the library and choose a number of books whose subjects (and pictures) appeal to them. Armed with stacks of books — from beginning readers to more informational texts — students bring them into the classroom and skim through them in a spirit of adventure. On a recent trip to the library, for example, one student chose books on Houdini, Lebron James, Legos, Colorado, and Texas. After doing the book-skimming thing, he chose Texas. For one thing, there were some Texas connections. Texas was his birthplace, so this was a buy-in, and he had fond early memories of Texas and family members still living there. Flipping through all the books, pictures, and captions he had collected told him more about Texas than other subject. So Texas it was.

Books with many pictures, captions, and headings work well for this approach. It is a good idea to allow any level of reading, even adult books. You are only using these resources to explore possibilities for a writing project. A wide variety makes for more options.

Sticky Note Notes

After skimming and choosing a subject, you will want your student to do a second thumb-through the chosen books armed with sticky notes. The sticky notes are for use as place holders for items of interest. An arrangement of these stickies later on will act as an outline of what the report will be about. (The resulting picture-based outline needs to be honored by teachers as well as the traditional verbal sequential outline.) Students should look closer at the pictures and captions, noting the titles. They should place sticky notes (or colored flags) on pages they want to come back to. A system of two colors, one for interest and another for "big information" helps them come back and organize. Finding what is interesting first is critical for picture thinkers, who move into their subject in stages, interest first. Remember, they do not digest information in a sequential way but are guided by their feelings.

An aside: you may want your student to use more than one resource for this writing project. A second trip to the library or the Internet should yield at least one other appealing book or article on the subject chosen. It can be thumbed through and marked with flags the same way as the first book of choice.

For the 10-year-old who chose Texas, the most interesting places in his book were Six Flags, the Space Museum, the Rio Grande, and the Aquarium. That is where he started. Then he discovered that alligators live in Texas and are sometimes run over by cars, and that became a new focal point. There was nothing yet about Texas history or the Alamo, but we did have a Texas buy-in. Cowboys were also a topic of interest. Now we had his attention, and his emotions were tied to the writing. There were exciting places to visit, there were alligators to save, and there were cowboys. He chose interesting places to write about first. (Incidentally, Crystal has found that taking a picture of the book and title page helps later when a bibliography needs to be included in the report. You can also assign the book a color, and simply put a dot of that color on any stickies or flags used with that book. This makes keeping track easier.)

At this point the student chose one of the books and picked other "big ideas" from it, using the table of contents. A table of contents provides a listing of the main ideas in a book. In the book on Texas, history, geography, people, climate, ways to make a living, industry, famous people, tourist attractions, and lots of information about the state bird, flag, flower, song were included. Students can be taught to look at the table of contents like a miner looking for nuggets. Then big ideas that appeal can be organized to create a plan for a report.

Using documentation boards to organize

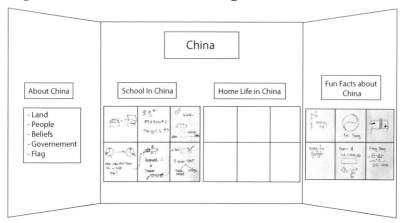

Picture thinkers struggle with organization, and a documentation board is large enough to hold their attention, where thoughts get lost in a folder on a messy desk. When they record their data in a notebook, students can only see one page at a time. This partial information makes it difficult to see how everything flows. It's hard to keep track of what has been done and what there is still to do. Using a large documentation board solves these problems.

The board holds the picture outline. Sticky notes containing freeze frame sketches can be arranged on the three panels of the board. Notes that have been taken can be cut up and also arranged on the board. To create a plan for a short introduction, a wide flow of information, and brief but dynamic ending, place stickies for the introduction in the narrower left-hand panel, those for the body of the report in the central panel, and those for conclusion in the narrow third panel. A child can easily stick the freeze frame sticky notes in an order, step back, and feel good about the report taking shape. It is also easy to see holes of information that need to be filled. So far, there has been a minimum of actual writing, but two major things have occurred. The writer is interested because he or she was able to choose the topic, and there is the beginning of a writing plan.

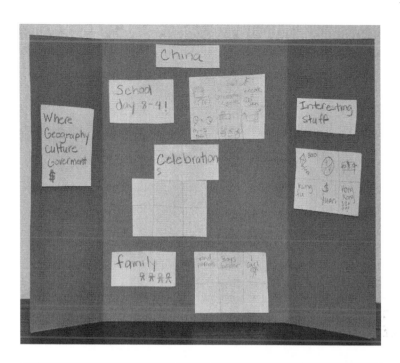

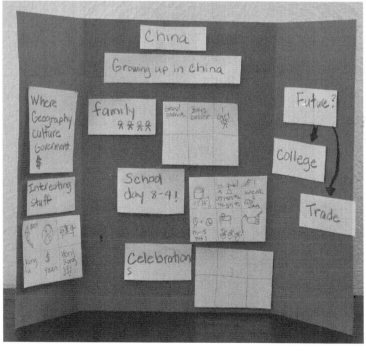

It is important that the sticky notes can be moved around. The top level of stickies shows the big ideas of the writing. Below the large ideas, assemble your "detail" stickies around each main idea. Then you can check to see if the details fit the main idea. You can also think of the main idea as a table top. That idea will need a minimum of 3-6 details stickies which make up the "legs" of the table. Too many "legs" and it's not going to balance; too few and the idea will not stand up. Practice will be needed to test out if the proposed main ideas are really the best big ideas.

This might be a good time for a brief student-teacher conference to go over the outline and general plan. There may be important holes. Or the plan may be very unbalanced. Perhaps it needs a different emphasis and would benefit from being re-titled. For example, "The State of Texas" may become "Neat Places to Visit in Texas." Some of the "big idea" stickies may need to be relocated. These may support a big idea already on the board or may be a detail needing a new big idea to go with.

It is essential to keep the student empowered and interested in the project, so teacher editorializing should not be heavy-handed. Spatial writers do best when their heart is in their subject. Focus on where their interest and enthusiasm lies and help them with a light touch to rearrange their writing plan to fit their interest.

Just as you would with your more traditional (sequential) students, you will be encouraging your spatial writers to create an order that makes sense, add details (picture notes), possibly seek out more information, and decide what important statements go in the conclusion. They will just be using picture notes (stickies) rather than word notes and a paper outline. The combination of freeze frame sticky notes and the doc board allows them to organize and see the entire topic at a glance. Stickies will stick to the board, but if they used paper, they can just cut up their notes and use tape to post them in the order they want. They can use the stickies as springboards for creating Freeze Frame details and cluster them around the big ideas on the document board. They then have prompts or reminders about writing the needed details in front of them instead of just in their head.

Adding details with freeze frame notes

One way to discover the details that go with the big pictures is to ask questions. You might post some major questions on the wall where everyone can see them. Or you might have two children get together and ask each other questions about freeze frame pictures each chooses to talk about. Some possible questions are:

Where is this?
What's going on?
Who lives here?
How did this start?
What surprised you about this?
How do people here make a living?
What is this person doing?
What are these people talking about?
What just happened?
Have you included enough sensory details?

The list is endless, but questions like this help the spatial writers include the needed details. The answers to such questions, which reveal what needs to be researched, become details that flesh out the big ideas. This process will need to be repeated several times as planning and research proceed together.

Freeze Frame Note Taking

Asking picture thinkers to keep track of and use word note cards is never a good idea. They never know how much information to add to each card, writing either too little or much too much. The cards are easily lost, hard to keep track of, and do not create a sequential outline that is useful to write from.

Expanding the idea of freeze frame to take picture notes is a winner. It is fast and efficient. It does not involve a lot of pre-writing, yet it effectively collects data for the first draft. A few words can be added to the freeze frames if wanted. Simple pictures are best, so the writer does not need to be an artist. Picture notes have proved to be useful even weeks later. They work as effectively as word notes. But it does take practice and there is a learning curve for creating effective picture notes. Some experimentation is needed for each child to learn what to put in a picture. Certainly not every sentence deserves a picture. It helps to think that a picture stands for an idea.

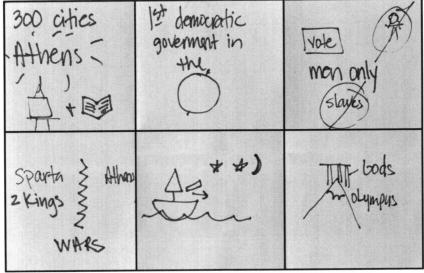

Having your students review their picture notes several days after they were created is a useful barometer. What does and does not make sense? Would more words or pictures have been helpful? Students should see what pictures work best for them.

To begin with, an easy way to take picture notes is to divide a piece of paper into six or eight sections. A different picture note goes in each section. Our writer on Texas found that by looking at maps, pictures, indexes, chapters about famous sites, collecting the information went quickly. For each picture, he added the page number and the color code for the book used, something that is easy to do. Many spatial learners will have phones with cameras. They can take a photo of the title page of the book and then color-code it with a dot or marker. Otherwise, information from each title page needs to be copied out and color-coded.

The process continues. As children come across something that seems important, they draw a picture of that idea in one of their page sections. The sections can then be cut apart and tentatively placed on a doc board with scotch tape or staples. Now the plan is beginning to take shape. There are stickies representing big ideas placed either at the beginning, middle, or end of the doc board. Around some stickies, there will be taped or stapled picture notes. A glance easily shows which big ideas have enough details surrounding them and which need more information.

We have an almost-complete, working model of a picture-based writing outline!

The Picture Writing Process

At this point, the picture thinker is ready to begin writing. The great thing about this method is that the writer may choose *any* big idea (even one of the details) to begin writing about. It is fine to begin anywhere, beginning, middle, or end. This choice means that they always have something to be writing about while the teacher checks progress around the classroom or confers with writers who have become stuck.

Using the freeze frame method insures focused, richly detailed writing about one subject at a time. Each piece of writing may be on a separate paper, or the writings may be cut apart to be reassembled, like a string of pearls, in order on the document board. Students can choose any frame to begin writing about.

Whatever picture is chosen first (usually it is something that feels exciting to the writer), the freeze frame method of writing is followed. It has become a positive writing habit: focus on one idea or paragraph totally, pulling in all the rich detail you can and making the words create a full experience. It is good to put the freeze frame sticky at the top of the page to hold focus and to use a new paper for writing about each sticky.

Each paragraph with a sticky at the top will have a statement about the big idea it represents. Then there will be several pages, each with its own picture note at the top, that give all the interesting, juicy facts that have been discovered about the big idea. The document board with its picture plan is always available for reference. Writers can see exactly how much of the whole they have completed and what else needs to be done.

Building Bridges

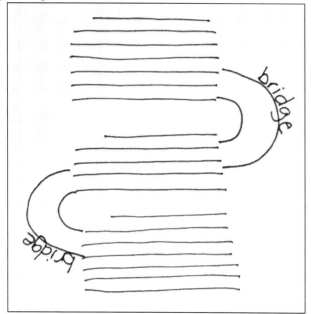

     The final product will need to be smoothly linked together with bridging words and phrases (In the first place, next, also, on the other hand, etc.). For picture thinkers, the emphasis is on creating a series of polished paragraphs and then constructing bridges to link them all up into a smoothly flowing piece of writing.

     There are two kinds of bridging words needed: bridges between paragraphs and connectors that lead smoothly from one sentence to another. As students approach the end of their project, it is a good time to look at the kind of words needed.

Four big ideas for choosing a subject for non-fiction writing:
1. Choice
     Provide a wide range of choice.
     Reporting about something means learning more about it, but it does not need to be dull or uninteresting.
     Your life is full of things that are interesting.
     You need to go with what is interesting.

Is there enough reading material to use the idea?
If they don't know anything about it, it is not in their
imagination.
2. Emotional connection
   a. Visualization—be in the moment you are writing
   about
   b. What are you connected to, or feel right about?
   c. Watch movies, visit museums, listen to radio, read
   books: "You are there"

3. Organic organization
   a. It is helpful to learn the organization of typical
   formats – book reports, etc.
   b. Graphic organizers may help; pick a pattern that
   speaks to you.

4. Encouragement— What is the idea here or use of language
that is exciting? Recognizing the strengths in the plan is vital
for engaging a picture thinker in the writing process.

Engage writers with topics that drive them. Thinking
and emotion are so intertwined in the right hemisphere that
picture thinkers can't generate an intellectual interest if they
don't feel anything about it. They really need a spark.

Organic organization for visual learners may be
different than using a set rubric. For example, when writing
about a person's life, they tend to follow the natural order,
birth to death, and include what feels significant to the writer.
One of their strengths is the ability to put themselves into
others' shoes, for example, seeing a situation from a Native
American point of view. If writing about big league football,
they would probably focus on their favorite teams and famous
stand-out points in football history. One help in organizing is
to consider what more would people want to know about this
subject. Writers might interview friends about what might be
important to write about.

Their organization will be more organic and personal, and that's all right. They will be working with how it holds together for them. You are going to get more brilliant writing when you let a picture thinker emphasis feelings, so teachers need to understand that their expectations need to be different. You might need two rubrics for grading—how interesting is it, use of language, does it flow?—and the regular rubric. A really good idea is to have the writer quantity the piece using an agreed-upon rubric.

VSLs are passionate about content that intrigues them and tells a unique story. They love situations of triumph over odds, of justice prevailing, tales full of adventure, and stories that are spicy with unexpected twists and turns. If given a choice to pick their own research subject, they usually are fairly willing to dig in. Listening to books on tape, gathering resources, conducting interviews, and looking at different points of view all stimulate their desire to explore.

Once their belly is full of information and they are satisfied, it may be still another challenge to get them to express what they learned about their subject. We often hear "Why do I need to write a report to prove that I know, read about, or understand the topic?" While gathering and learning information—whether it was from the history channel, videos, books, or interviews— is fascinating, retelling the info is not quite as much fun, nor does it feel necessary. It is the teacher's job to find a real audience to share the information with, perhaps through videotaping or staging a coffee shop performance, complete with musical jamming, to which parents are invited.

In the unfolding of the story or report, lines blur between significant and insignificant information. What is important to repeat and report? The fun of learning sometimes gets lost in the necessity of providing proof of what has been learned. Many teachers have students write historical fiction, science, fiction, etc., where fact is woven with fiction, allowing the writer and reader to become part of the story. These types of assignments offer the ability to be creative, join the information as it happens, and use all of the senses to describe a scene as if you were living it.

Each time we encourage students to experience, even in their imaginations, what a significant time period might have been like or to step into the shoes of a particular character or well-known historical person, they are building new experience. They have the opportunity to evaluate and sense the material, visualize and conceptualize at a much deeper level than usual. They take away information that has become relevant to them. This is really different from reading information that is outside their experience, therefore not significant, and easily forgotten. If they are familiar with visualization techniques, they may be able to use this tool to understand a topic they do not have any personal knowledge of. However, they will need some concrete details to jumpstart the visualization process.

Just as we engage the reluctant writer with writing from the heart, the same strategy can be used when writing non-fiction. Once we have engaged our students and provided stimulating subjects to explore, engaging questions to be answered, and " what ifs" to be considered, we have gone far to capture the heart and mind of a reluctant picture thinker. Give them something exciting to sink their teeth into, and they are hooked.

Encouragement- A Necessary Ingredient

Many picture thinkers are reluctant writers because they have received many papers riddled with corrections, and the feedback rarely highlights their good ideas. The draft work is often beset with incorrect grammar, spelling, and missing details. These writers are discouraged with the writing process from the beginning. They need gentle handling to regain their confidence.

Encouragement goes a long way in developing writing stamina. I have witnessed reluctant writers become voracious writers because a teacher encouraged their ideas, honored their stories, and looked for the strengths in their writing. Picture thinkers will be overwhelmed with the amount of information they need to acquire in a research project, and providing positive encouragement along the way helps keep their motors humming.

A recent reluctant writer has bloomed and sees himself as a writer under the expert tutelage of a wise teacher who understood how fragile he felt about writing. She also understood that he had a wonderful imagination, so she helped him capture his ideas on paper, choosing juicy words and phrases that sounded exactly like him. She honored his writing with an expressive reading to the class of his work. This same reluctant writer is now coming in at recess to spend his recess time writing! He is a writer and now he believes this of himself. As Crystal said to her, "You have hatched a writer." Positive feedback, appropriate challenge, and honoring the product are equally valuable in fostering any new skill.

Freeze Frame to the Rescue Again

Using the same strategy you used to engage beginning or reluctant writers to write from the heart, you can once again use freeze frame to help them organize what is important to write about. Additionally, writers can remain flexible using this tool. They have the flexibility and the freedom to change that may be needed to nail down a specific writing topic.

A writer can organize information in a variety of methods. If a class is studying a subject, such as historic explorers, big questions about the topic can be set up at information centers. Time lines of explorers' lives might be broken up by time period. A comparison and contrast system can be used posting the larger themes to be compared and contrasted. The idea is to get the large pieces of content, themes, and events decided upon near the beginning of the project. This way teachers will be able to better guide the research process and discovery of significant information. The important ideas that writers first began with may change as they learn more about their topic, and these changes should be expected. If students know that they have the ability to change their plan as they learn, this takes away some anxiety. Giving your students freedom to change their mind and negotiate aspects of an assignment facilitates their independence, supports their thinking process, and motivates them.

Large ideas the freeze frame way

Choice and freedom in organizing the content gives students the opportunity to begin anywhere in the assignment. Freeze frame will keep the plan in place so they can go back and finish an area of study. Once students have decided which areas need to be covered, they can use the freeze frame technique to sort and organize their topics. Or, a writer can organize the known aspects of a topic as a plan of facts and information that require more research, again using freeze frame. The teacher's part is to make clear the purpose and learning goals of the assignment, information that will make the organization process easier to accomplish.

There are many graphic organizer resources for non-fiction writing. Again, documentary boards are great for providing a big picture overview of the whole plan. A free-standing board is useful in organizing the non-fiction writing as well as fiction pieces.

Juicy Scraps

This term was first coined by the writer, Judy Blume, who said that she was fortunate in her junior year to have a teacher that encouraged creativity and each student's individual approach. She said that her teacher did not like all of her works, but encouraged and pushed her to become a better writer. Juicy scraps may be small, but they are significant moments of a story or essay. Such writing stems from the talk going on inside the mind that narrates the very moment in time. They can also be a short writing piece that allows the writer to find his or her vision, voice, humor, or expression of the senses in a way that allows the reader to be in the moment with the writer. Readers of juicy scraps can experience something from the inside out.

Bringing the Subject to Life

If the writer has no prior experience with the topic, visiting museums and watching movies about the subject and its time era can help make those connections. Listening to books on tape prior to the start of the writing is also helpful. Other connections like music, clothing, food, and religion can help build experience for the writer to connect with and draw upon.

Using the table of contents in each book chosen, writers will find a listing of big ideas. If they are researching a state, for example, they are likely to find such subheadings as History, Geography, Climate, Ways to make a living, Industry, Famous people from the area, and Interesting places to visit. There will also be lots of information about the state flag, bird, flower, song, etc. Many of these big ideas can be transferred to the freeze frame format and used to create a picture outline.

Big to Small

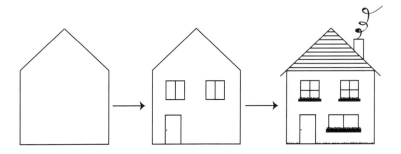

Describing something usually works best if you start your plan with the largest piece. Headings can give you information on where to begin organizing the facts. Sometimes a few leading questions help the planning, such as:

What are we talking about?
Where is it?
What does it look like?
Who lives there?
What are the most interesting or surprising things that you have discovered?
How did it start?
How do people make a living?

The list of ideas is endless, but the important thing is that these questions become triggers for searching out what is important. Writers need to know that they can change their mind and the arrangement of the sections if needed. Once they have an initial list of ideas to investigate, they can sketch them on colored paper or arrange sticky notes as headings with space below for the notes that go with each.

Writing from big to small also includes the idea of a main or leading sentence within a paragraph. The big idea is expressed in the leading sentence, which is usually the first

sentence, while the other sentences in the paragraph fill in the details. It is also possible, at a later stage of writing, that the main idea may be expressed in the last sentence. Then it becomes a summing up
of what the paragraph was about.

Organizing the Big Ideas: Documentation Boards

Picture thinkers struggle with organization. It is hard for them to keep track of their notes, loose papers, bibliography information, and recognizing what is still left to be finished. When they record their information in a notebook, it is difficult to see how the paper flows; as information is usually recorded randomly in various sections. It also makes it hard to know what sections have not been covered. Using a large documentation board solves many of these issues. It helps the writer see what has been done and what is left to do. It becomes the outline, as it has the titles of the "big ideas" that can be moved around, and allows the writer flexibility with starting at any point in the project with "place holders" keeping track of the next steps.

The use of science document boards that stand up and have three sides is very useful to organize the information collected. The dark colored boards seem to work best, as most of the notes are on white paper, and one can easily see if anything is missing. You can use sticky notes or paper stapled onto the board to organize the large ideas. It helps if they can be moved around later if you decide to. The notion of writing from large to small seems to be helpful when deciding what information to begin with.

The first section and the last section of the documentation board are narrower than the middle. This is a natural fit for the introduction and the conclusion. It also neatly shows that the bulk of the information is in the wide middle. After writers have chosen their big ideas, they can arrange them on the doc board and see if the organization works. They can always change the order as they collect the data. Now they are ready to begin their research.

Freeze Frame Note Taking or "Picture Notes"

The elephant is the largest animal in the world that lives on land. A full-grown elephant may have a weight of about four tons and may be nine feet tall. Because elephants are so large, they have no natural enemies other than man. Since elephants have so few enemies, they are usually easy to get along with and almost always act friendly.

Elephants usually live in herds with around thirty members of all ages. A female, or lady elephant, is called a cow. The herd usually has a cow as its leader, who is in charge of all the other elephants. During the hottest part of the day, the herd will huddle together and attempt to find shade. Near sundown the entire herd usually goes to a nearby river or lake for a drink. Elephants normally continue to stay together in a herd for most of their lives.

From the Ekwall Shankar reading Inventory

Asking a picture thinker to keep track of and use note cards is never a good idea. They never know how much information to add to each card. Either it is too little or way too much. The cards are easily lost and hard to keep track of, and, because the main information does not stand out, they do not create a sequential outline that is useful to write from.

Using the idea of "freeze frame" to take picture notes is a good place to start. It does not involve a lot of pre-writing, although it effectively collects the data until the first draft. Taking picture notes instead of writing is fast and efficient. The writer does not need to be artistic as the simplest pictures are the best. This method takes practice. It has to be tried many times to get the right amount of drawing and words so that the frames can be useful even weeks later. Having your students review their picture notes several days after they were created is a useful barometer. Was the information easy to assess? What did not make sense? Would more words or more pictures have been helpful? Using a full sheet of paper that has been sectioned into six to eight areas is enough to capture the important ideas to begin with. Each page should be color-coded to match the book it deals with. For picture or short phrase, the page number should be listed to aid looking up more details or in creating a bibliography, if that is needed.

Basically, what you are doing for your students is:

- Building motivation
- Encouraging them to write about what interests them
- Introducing them to great tools like freeze frame and doc boards to organize and see a topic as a whole.

Drawing Apps are very useful for computers, I-pads, etc- , apps such as noteability, doodlebug"-allow you to draw and save to your screen!

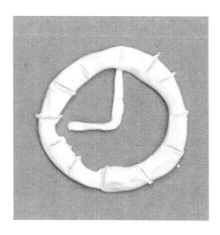

Chapter 7
Time and Organization For Picture Thinkers

Most picture thinkers struggle with time and organization. They have trouble keeping track of time, being on time, and using their time efficiently. Their sense of time is lacking. The minute they get into their imagination, or are absorbed in a game, book, art, or some other passion, time ceases to exist. They cannot judge if two minutes, twenty minutes, or two hours have passed.

Picture thinkers also have a difficult time estimating how long something will take. Almost always they underestimate the needed amount of time. That is because they can visualize the final product, and they usually do not anticipate any snags. Thirty minutes to write a draft seems reasonable. If everything went as planned, and the reading was completed to write a the draft, and they had already formulated the main points and organized the writing in their mind, and they could type at least 30 wpm, then 30 minutes might be reasonable. But how often is all of this in place?

Usually life has other ideas. The books you need at the library are checked out, you cannot find the article you read on line, you have a dental appointment you forgot about, you leave the requirements for the paper at school, your computer won't cooperate, your printer is out of ink, or you watched just 30 minutes more T.V. than you planned and now its bedtime....the list goes on and on. This is a frequent pattern for picture thinkers.

Developing a Sense of Time

Here are some ideas to nurture a barely emergent sense of time. It helps to use experience to build in a sense of time passing. Talk over with your child or student about just how long it takes to listen to a song on the radio, or how long a half-hour TV sitcom will last. These are good places to begin. You can do exercises with your class to see how long five minutes really is. Start them working on something and ask them to look up at the clock when they think five minutes have gone by but not before. Everyone is always surprise to find out that five minutes is longer than they had imagined. You can buy a device called a Time Timer, which will mark an amount of time, say 15 minutes, by a colored segment of the clock face, which gradually reduces as time passes. This is great for picture thinkers, because time's movement can easily be seen.

Estimated vs. Actual Time

Here are some ideas to help your picture thinker students develop their time sense. Have them find out for themselves just how long some common actions take. Consider the following questions about how long a reading assignment might take for them.

- How long does it take to read a page?
- How long does it take to read a non-fiction page of text?

- How long does it take to find books/resources?
- How long does it take to write a one page draft?
- How long does it take to write a 5 page draft?
- How long does it take to edit a page of writing?
- How long does it take to eat a meal?

To get an average of how long it takes to read a page, students need to find a book that does not have any pictures and they are reading comfortably — this needs to be at their independent reading level. They should do at least three one-page readings and time each one. Then they should calculate the average for the three readings. This process provides a sense of how long it takes to read a page. Based on this information, they can predict how long it will take for them to read a chapter or a book at that same reading level.

The same can be done for a text book – this will take longer than reading a story. A text book has so much new information that it takes longer to sort out the important information and take notes. Also, a page of math is going to be read at a different speed than a social studies text. The reading rate also needs to be based on what is comfortable for the individual.

Banking Time

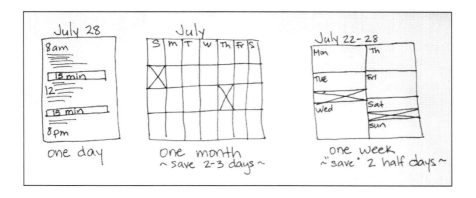

Banking or saving time is as important as saving money. Most people never have enough time, but saving time for a picture thinker is an essential, invaluable tool for a less stressful life.

Banking time means adding time cushions to your plan for a day. This is especially important for picture thinkers to do, because they visualize everything going optimally, with no glitches, no interruptions, and no crises. That is not real life!

Bank time daily—at least 15 minutes a day (more is even better). You need a breather or a small amount of time each day just to play catch up with yourself. Twice a day is helpful—once mid-morning and once mid-afternoon. This helps to refocus and re-prioritize the contents of the day, review the goals for the day, and also allows for the unexpected, which you can actually expect to happen. On a weekly basis, schedule half a day to save throughout the week Monthly, schedule 2-3 days to save as catch- up days in which you do not schedule any other commitments or activities. You will be amazed at the amount of stress reduction wise planning can bring about.

Planning That Works for You

Every individual is different with different energy levels, ability to focus, and needs. You want your planning to work for you, not against you. Really analyze yourself, thinking about such factors as your best time of day to work. Are you a night owl, a morning person, or someone who takes a while to get going but really cranks out work in the late morning? Build you plan around your strengths. Sometimes people have a small ritual they need to carry out before starting to work, like eating a small snack, or sharpening all their pencils. Within reason, such habits can be helpful, but watch out for sheer avoidance of work!

Some other factors to consider in your planning are:

a. How long can you work before you need a break?
b. What kinds of breaks do you need?
c. Is music helpful or not? What about smells? It is also really helpful to be clear about your goals for this work session.

Summing It All Up

"Everybody is a genius. But if you judge a fish by its ability to climb a tree, it will live its whole life believing that it is stupid." --Albert Einstein

During the last 12 years of working with visual thinkers in particular, I, Crystal, noticed that each person I worked with has suffered loss of self-esteem and a sense of alienation as a result of not fitting into the typical classroom learning experience. In reflecting on their education years, many felt a kind of prejudice towards their learning differences as well-meaning people tried to help them learn like word thinkers. The message this sent was: You aren't good enough until you can learn like the rest of the class. If not, they had to endure the pain of failed tests, or loss of points for not getting all of the work completed. Many have heard the phrase, "You just aren't working to your potential and you are not trying hard enough!" In a time when we have more information about learning differences, we are still missing the mark on these visual students.

As wonderfully inquisitive and creative as most of these individuals are, they have a sense of failure or feel broken somehow. If they are so wonderfully intelligent, then why can't they seem to do the basics required of them in the classroom. These creative thinkers do not need to be fixed. Rather, we are suggesting they need a different angle into their learning, a shift in the way instruction is applied in the classroom to accommodate these visual thinkers and processors. If we insist on assessing their knowledge in a strictly sequential manner, we are missing the opportunity to harness creativity, intuition, and vision. As educators we need to broaden our view of knowledge to embrace all these students have to offer.

Adults will frequently say they feel broken or hang onto those defining moments when they realized they were different because they could not spell like everyone else, they struggled with reading, struggled with writing, struggled with test taking, note taking, organization, time management, and so forth. Many students develop elaborate compensation strategies to get by and continue to use those strategies to hide their difficulties. We have all heard of creative, intelligent people who struggled or did not fit the school mold, yet became famous in their on right as inventors, artists, computer scientists, and CEOs. These are the fortunate ones, but for every fortunate one, there are a crowd of visual learners who still struggle into adulthood because of the injuries they suffered as student, both at our hands as educators and their peers. It is a basic human need to be understood and supported to be one's best.

One student once told me that if there were schools for visual kids and word thinkers attended, there, then the word thinkers would be in special education!

There you have it — the big picture of the road to academic success for picture thinkers. Most of the suggestions we propose call for minimal changes in your classroom and make for a more creative classroom climate. As you try out some of these ideas, you may well wish to revise our Ten Tips for teaching visual-spatial learners with your own tips. That would be fantastic! We would love to hear from you regarding new tips and successful strategies that made your classroom come alive. Do contact us at **www.visualspatial.org** with your comments.

.

Bibliography

Ashton-Warner, Sylvia. *Spinster, a Novel*. New York: Simon and Schuster, 1959. Print.

Ashton-Warner, Sylvia. *Teacher*. New York: Simon and Schuster, 1963. Print.

Bell, Nanci. *Visualizing and Verbalizing: For Language Comprehension and Thinking*. Paso Robles, CA: Academy of Reading Publications, 1991. Print.

Buzan, Tony. *Mind Mapping*. Harlow: BBC Active, 2006. Print.

Cannon, Janell. *Stellaluna*. San Diego: Harcourt Brace Jovanovich, 1993. Print.

Davis, Ronald D. *The Gift of Dyslexia*. New York: Perigee Book, 1997. Print.

De, Mille Richard. *Put Your Mother on the Ceiling: Children's Imagination Games*. New York: Penguin, 1976. Print.

Freed, Jeffrey, and Laurie Parsons. *Right-brained Children in a Left-brained World: Unlocking the Potential of Your ADD Child*. New York, NY: Simon & Schuster, 1997. Print.

Galyean, Beverly. *Mind Sight: Learning through Imaging*. Long Beach, CA: Center for Integrative Learning, 1983. Print.

Gardner, Howard. *Multiple Intelligences: The Theory in Practice*. New York, NY: Basic, 1993. Print.

"Learn Almost Anything for Free." Khan Academy. Web. 23 Sept. 2012. <http://www.khanacademy.org/>.

Margulies, Nancy, and Nusa Maal. *Mapping Inner Space: Learning and Teaching Visual Mapping*. Tucson, AZ: Zephyr, 2002.

"Mister Numbers Pattern Play Math." Mister Numbers Right Brain Math. Web. 23 Sept. 2012. <http://eztimestable.com/>.

Ornstein, Robert E. *The Right Mind: Making Sense of the Hemispheres*. New York: Harcourt Brace, 1997. Print.

Shanker, James L., and Eldon E. Ekwall. *Reading Inventory*. Boston: Allyn and Bacon, 2000. Print.

Silverman, Linda Kreger. *Upside-down Brilliance: The Visual-spatial Learner*. Denver, CO: DeLeon Pub., 2002. Print.

"Visual Learning Overview." Inspiration Software, Inc. Web. 23 Sept. 2012. <http://www.inspiration.com/>.

"Voice Thread - Conversations in the Cloud." Voice Thread – Conversations in the Cloud. Web. 23 Sept. 2012. <http://voicethread.com/>.

Appendix

The Visual-Spatial Learner in School

Betty Maxwell

There are two main ways of organizing the world. These are *spatial* (using space) and *sequential* (using time). Spatial people tend to use space as a whole. They get a sudden "aha" recognition of patterns or significant relationships that they see in their mind. Sequential people organize information by following a logical sequence of steps to a conclusion. Even when they are organizing space, they do it in a linear, orderly way, such as writing from left to right, or building an outline from the top down. There are also two basic learning styles: *visual-spatial* and *auditory-sequential.*

Auditory-sequential learners are good listeners. They do well with a step-by-step presentation of information. They process what they hear quickly and are usually able to express themselves well when they speak. Most schools teach in this auditory-sequential style. They break down complex information into small bits and present the easier steps first. Then they gradually move into the more complex and difficult parts.

In contrast, visual-spatial learners (VSLs) are fine observers. They think in images and usually see things as a whole. It may take a while for them to express themselves verbally, because they have to translate their images and thoughts into words. Sometimes it is hard for them to find the right words. Their thinking and emotions are very entwined. Their different learning style often makes them feel out-of-step in traditional school settings. Visual-spatial learners are not all the same. They are a varied group that includes persons talented in art, science, mechanics, technology, computers, math concepts, and understanding of human relationships—anything that uses strong visualization skills.

Recognition of the visual-spatial learning style is new in our society and it is not as well understood as the more established auditory-sequential style. This instrument is designed to help identify and understand visual-spatial learners. A cluster of VSL traits is needed for identification. The more traits, the more strongly spatial a learner will be. Some of the characteristics might also belong to sequential learners, because there is no dividing line between these two natural ways of organizing the world.

We have identified 8 basic categories, 32 *positive traits* (bold, coded with plus signs) clustered under these 8 categories, and 71 *potential school problems* (coded with minus signs.) Many VSLs are successful in school because they have good sequential abilities to complement their strong spatial abilities. They exhibit the 32 positive characteristics without many of the related school problems. Those VSLs who have problems in school usually have sequential weaknesses. When the degree of sequential weakness is severe, the student may suffer from a learning disability. However, "school problems" as used here does not necessarily mean a learning disability. It is necessary to refer a child to a qualified examiner to determine if a learning disability exists.

Identifying Characteristics of Visual-Spatial Learners

Are Visual, Not Auditory

Have a strong visual learning style.
> May find it hard to follow spoken directions, explanations or instructions, unless pictures, charts or other visual aids are also used.

Some can pay attention only to a teacher who uses lots of visual aids and has a dramatic presentation style. Speaking in a monotone is especially hard for them to follow.

Are excellent visualizers and learn best through visual imagery.

Need to visualize in order to follow and remember, but may not be aware they can do this. Some may need help and practice in visualizing.

Think primarily in images instead of words.

May need extra time to translate their images and ideas into words.

May know the answer but not be able to get it out quickly when asked a quick response question. (Need a longer response time.)

If their eyes are looking upward, they may be searching for an image. If they are interrupted, the image can easily be lost.

Learn from seeing better than from listening.

May have trouble learning from listening alone.

May need to look away from a speaker in order to focus their listening attention, because looking and listening at the same time is too much.

May have had many ear infections when young. This can result in problems of processing what they hear. Sometimes this kind of inattention may be mistaken for attention deficit disorder.

Remember lectures best through their own kind of note-taking, which may be pictures, doodles or webs showing relationships.

They may try to capture complex ideas with "chicken scratch" notations.

They may be restricted from "doodling" by teachers who do not understand what they are doing.

Note-taking may be a real problem, especially in middle and high school. They often cannot listen and write.

Are Spatial, Not Sequential

Are more space oriented and less time oriented. (For example, when very young, may know how to get to a favorite place even when the route is complicated. Or may know exactly what rooms are above or below them in a large building. But they won't be dressed on time or ready to go.)

Have little sense of time. Scheduling is not a strength.

May have a terrible time meeting deadlines and need help with organizational strategies.

Reach correct conclusions without taking any visible steps.

May not be able to show their work.

Because they don't know the steps they took (if any) to get their answer, they may not be confident about being able to do it again.

May be accused of cheating by teachers because they cannot show their steps.

May blurt out an answer because they are afraid they will lose their idea and not be able to reconstruct it.

Are natural non-linear processors. They are global thinkers.

May not learn readily when material is presented in the usual sequential order.

May have a lot of difficulty following someone else's line of thinking.

May not become automatic in left-to-right reading. They may have difficulty remembering right from left.

May reverse words or letters or numbers and this problem may persist throughout school years.

May not learn to read directly from phonics instruction. May need to apply analytic phonics after learning many whole words by sight.

May solve problems by starting at the end and working backward or at the middle and working toward both ends. This may not be acceptable in a class situation.

Are Holistic, Not Detail Oriented

Are whole-to-part learners who need to see the big picture first. They grasp concepts and systems all at once and only later learn the details.

Need a frame of reference to help them in their learning process.

Putting information in a larger context is essential for them to absorb new material.

May fail to remember details unless they are helped to see the big picture first or are given a framework to fit details into so that it all makes sense to them.

May score poorly on tests because they fail to focus on small details.

Have much difficulty learning and remembering isolated bits of information.

Often grasp a concept or process with only one or two examples—the "aha" phenomenon.

Many examples of the same kind don't make a concept any clearer to them and may turn off their thinking processes. If they don't get the idea with the first few examples, they need a different approach, a new angle.

Grasp ideas as a complete whole, with all the parts connected.

May be upset when their ideas are analyzed, revised, or "improved" because it feels as if the whole idea has been destroyed.

May need to visualize something as complete before beginning a project.

May not turn in a school assignment because it feels incomplete — only a part of what they see as a bigger whole.

May find it hard to take tests until they feel they have an understanding of the whole.

See the interrelationships between ideas. This is very important to them.

Have difficulty separating out main and supporting ideas or summarizing.

May have difficulty with multiple choice tests because they can see ways in which many answers could be right. If asked, they can support these answers.

May find the expected answers in true/false tests too simplistic. They see the situations as more complex.

Are Focused On Ideas, Not Format

Continually build permanent frameworks of ideas instead of memorizing rote information that is easily forgotten.

Do not learn through drill, practice or repetition.

Learn best when information is meaningful to them. May need to ask a series of questions to understand fully.

Rote memorization is a weakness.

Are much more interested in ideas than in the particulars of their presentation.

Are likely to make errors in computation, grammar, spelling and punctuation.

Are oriented to the process, not the product.

What is important to them is their own understanding of an idea. They may be less interested in demonstrating their mastery to someone else in the form of a product.

They may know much more than they show.

Seek Patterns

Look for patterns and connections. Often they will find patterns no one has noticed before. Sometimes they will notice connections between things that other people see as quite different.

May have difficulty learning unless they see a pattern or can make connections with something they already know.

May find these patterns, connections, and explorations more interesting than what is being taught. May find it hard to hold their focus on narrowly focused topics.

Are Divergent, Not Convergent

Are divergent thinkers, preferring solutions that are more creative.

May be actually unaware of the more usual methods of problem-solving or classification—or they may be unable to use these because they have things framed in a different way.

Are highly imaginative and creative.

May have their own creative approach which conflicts with a teacher's conventional approach.

May be artistic.

May be a persistent doodler or sketcher, even during teacher presentations.

Tend to be rhythmic and musical.

May be a finger drummer. May need rhythm and music to enhance learning. May actually do homework better with the radio or TV on.

May be inventive and have mechanical aptitude.

May daydream, visualizing machines or inventions rather than the subject at hand.

May require a hands-on approach to learning.

May be used to setting their own agenda for learning because they learn in their own way.

May find it hard to leave a project and move on to the next scheduled thing.

Are Sensitive and Intense

May have acutely developed senses.

Can be distracted easily by a variety of sounds, movements, etc.

It may be difficult for them to ignore things in the environment that probably wouldn't bother others, such as bright lights, noises of motors, fans, etc.

Respond very readily to many things in their environment.

Are easily irritated by many conditions, such as wool or nubby socks, clothing tags, certain foods, changes in air pressure, environmental chemicals, even the presence of others around them.

May exhibit a great deal of energy.

May need to move their bodies or their hands to learn, think, or talk fluently.

Are highly sensitive emotionally. Learn best when emotionally involved.

May need emotional involvement in order to learn.

Do not respond well to criticism, even when it is intended to be constructive.

May need what they learn to be personally significant to them.

May be highly aware of other people's feelings.

May be aware of unspoken disapproval by a teacher or other students.

Are able to focus extremely intently on a topic.

May have trouble moving from one task to another.

Display Variable "Asynchronous" Development

Think faster than their hands can capture, because mental development is often ahead of fine motor skills.

May have illegible handwriting with poorly formed letters. Sometimes this is a jumble of cursive and manuscript letters without spacing between words.

May never feel comfortable with cursive writing and choose to print, even as adults.

May be frustrated with writing assignments and unwilling to write down their thoughts. May be unable to capture thoughts in writing.

May be spatially gifted and "verbally inconvenienced."*

May be afraid of public speaking and other situations where quick responses are needed.

May have trouble finding the right words to express their ideas.

May not be able to retrieve words quickly enough to explain themselves when asked to justify their ideas. This can be very embarrassing.

Often succeed at more complex tasks yet continue to have difficulties with simple tasks.

May have found it difficult to memorize math facts, yet can do well with more complex mathematical concepts.

May write at a much lower level than they speak because they are afraid of misspelling words.

May be frustrated and even turned off from learning by being held to mastery of simple material when they are capable of excelling at complex work. (This is important.)

May have wide discrepancies on different portions of IQ tests. Scores may be much higher on spatial relations (e.g., Block Design) and measures of verbal abstract reasoning (e.g., Vocabulary, Similarities, Comprehension, Information) than on measures of attention and sequential memory (e.g., Arithmetic, Digit Span, Coding).

If discrepancies exceed 9 points, learning disabilities may be indicated.

*Lohman, D. F. (1994). Spatially gifted, verbally inconvenienced. In N. Colangelo, S. G. Assouline, & D. L. Ambroson (Eds.). *Talent development: Proceedings from the 1993 Henry B. and Jocelyn Wallace National Research Symposium on Talent Development* (pp. 251-264). Dayton, OH: Ohio Psychology Press.

Made in the USA
San Bernardino, CA
22 August 2014